LET'S WA

**Series Edit

Southern England

Don Philpott

Line drawings by Brian Pearce

JAVELIN BOOKS

POOLE · NEW YORK · SYDNEY

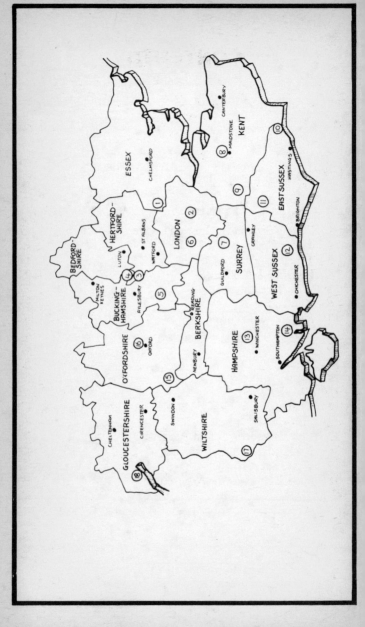

CONTENTS

First published in the UK 1987 by Javelin Books,
Link House, West Street, Poole, Dorset, BH15 1LL

Copyright © 1987 Javelin Books

Distributed in Australia by
Capricorn Link (Australia) Pty Ltd,
PO Box 665, Lane Cove, NSW 2066

British Library Cataloguing in Publication Data

Philpott, Don
  Southern England. —(Let's walk there!)
  1. England —Description and travel —
  1971- —Guide-books
  I. Title   II. Series
  914.22′04858   DA650

ISBN 0 7137 1775 0

Cartography by Ron Rigby

Cover picture:
Tower Bridge courtesy of The British Tourist
Authority, Britain on View (BTA/ETB)

Typeset by Inforum Ltd, Portsmouth
Printed in Great Britain by Cox & Wyman Ltd, Reading, Berks

INTRODUCTION

As worthwhile as any walk might be, it becomes doubly appealing if it takes you to some place of special interest. The nine books in this series, covering England, Scotland and Wales were conceived to describe just such walks.

A full description of the walk's objective is given at the start of each chapter. The objectives are diverse, giving a wide choice. Most are non-seasonal, and involve little walking in themselves once you are there.

Following the description of the objective, each section of the walk is clearly described, and a specially drawn map makes route-finding straightforward. As well as detailing the route, the authors describe many subsidiary points of interest encountered along the way.

The walks are varied and easy to follow. None of them is too taxing, except in the severest weather. Most are circular, returning you to your car at the starting point. Family walkers with young children will find plenty of shorter routes to suit their particular needs, whilst those with longer legs can select from more substantial walks.

The routes have been carefully chosen to include only well-established routes, and readers will certainly increase the enjoyment which they and others derive from the countryside if they respect it by following the Country Code.

Bruce Bedford
Series Editor

Walk 1
QUEEN ELIZABETH'S HUNTING LODGE
EPPING FOREST, ESSEX
6 miles

Queen Elizabeth's Hunting Lodge is a delightful timbered building dating from the early sixteenth century. It is thought to have been built in 1510, when Epping Forest was one of the largest Royal hunting forests in England, stretching to more than 12,000 acres. Because of its nearness to London and the abundance of game, especially deer and wild boar, it was popular with various monarchs; the lodge itself is understood to have been re-named after Queen Elizabeth I had stayed there. Today the lodge is a museum devoted to the life of animals, birds and plants in Epping Forest, and man's association with them. It is open Wednesday to Sunday throughout the year, and on bank holidays. There is a modest charge for adults but accompanied children are admitted free.

Epping Forest, which still covers about 6,000 acres, was purchased on behalf of the public in 1882. It has inspired many of the country's finest artists and authors; the hornbeams in particular gave inspiration to the sculptor and artist Sir Jacob Epstein, and the poet Tennyson lived at nearby High Beach.

Today the forest is one large leisure area with numerous paths and bridleways. A mile wide, it runs for four miles north to south; the trees are mixed deciduous, mostly thorn, oak and pollarded hornbeams. The area is particularly well-known to birdwatchers, and is one of the strongholds of the redstart. In the summer you can also try to spot the elusive

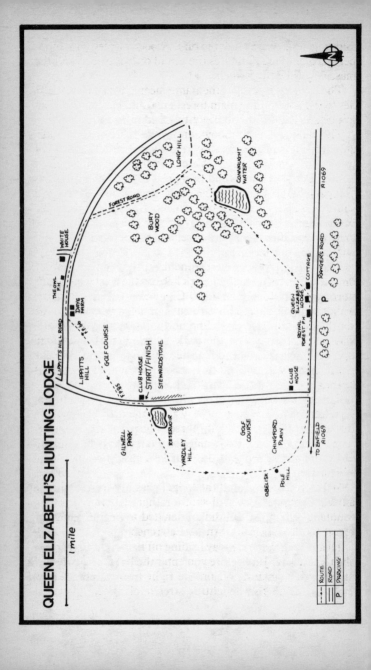

QUEEN ELIZABETH'S HUNTING LODGE

1 mile

- ------- ROUTE
- ———— ROAD
- P PARKING

nightingale as well as the tree pipit, wood warbler, grasshopper warbler (which imitates the sound of that insect) and the massively billed hawfinch.

The town of Epping – the name means 'forest clearing' – lies to the north of the main forest area, and has long been an important halt on the journey to London from the north.

The walk is easy to follow, and while there are a few ups and down it is not taxing. There are some large expanses of water, notably Connaught Water and the reservoir south of Gilwell Park, so young children need to be kept in sight as you pass them. Because much of the area is wooded, it takes some time to dry out after rain, so boots are a good idea. The bridleways are also well used by horses which can churn the ground up. Binoculars are essential as the area is rich in wildlife, especially birds.

The walk starts at Sewardstonebury, south of junction 26 on the M25. It is possible to park here on the road which runs north of the A1069 Enfield to Chigwell road. To start the walk take the little road which runs beside a reservoir to the south, with Gilwell Park to the north. Then take the bridleway at the entrance to the park, bearing right and going uphill. This takes you to Yardley Hill where you take the path to your left, marked by a stake at the junction where it branches off from the main track.

This path takes you to Pole Hill and an obelisk where you turn left again to make your way along the path which skirts the southern flanks of a golf course. The path brings you out near a road junction. Go straight on along the Ranger's Road (A1069) and the lodge is on your left, just after the Royal Forest Inn.

When you have visited the lodge, pass between it and the adjacent cottage. You will spot a rather elaborate drinking fountain behind the buildings, donated to people using the forest by Sir Edward Durning-Lawrence.

Head along the bridleway leading off half-right making for the trees ahead. Just before you enter the trees, you will see a small path branching off on the right from the bridleway. Follow this to the delightful stretch of water known as

Epping Forest: the majesty of trees in one of Britain's oldest Royal forests

Connaught Water. Stroll round the lake – there is a good path with plenty of seats from which to watch the birds. A good place for a picnic.

Leave the path round Connaught Water by a well-used path running off from the north-east corner of the lake. This track, which crosses over a number of small streams, is also used by cyclists and joggers and can be quite muddy after rain. It takes you out to a private forest road which you follow to the left, walking along the grass, until you reach a public road. Follow the left-hand forks of this main road for about one mile, but note that it is possible to walk on paths running through the trees parallel to it.

You will pass the Field Studies Training Centre and the large White House, then the road winds uphill to a cluster of houses and the Owl public house. Pass the police training camp on your left, a mobile home park on your right, and you should then see the signpost for the footpath no.66 to Sewardstone Green. Take this path, past a memorial to

10

anti-aircraft gunners who protected London during the last war and out across another golf course.

The path skirts the various holes and you should turn left again at the signpost for footpath no.85. The path becomes a little less clear but you should be able to follow it to the road on your right on to which you emerge just north of Sewardstonebury.

The great thing about this walk is that you can have a marvellous time watching the wildlife. The whole area teems with birds and you can sit and watch wrens, bullfinches, hawfinches, pied wagtails, tits and hordes of others. I saw a kestrel standing guard on one bush and was able to watch it for several minutes before it swooped silently away. The area is also rich in other wildlife; keep an eye open for grey squirrels, mice, voles, and even weasels darting about in search of prey.

If you don't want such a long walk you can take any of the bridleways or paths that criss-cross the forest. Provided that you have some sense of direction you should not get lost, even devising your own route.

Walk 2
TOWER BRIDGE
LONDON
4½ miles

This is a super walk right in the heart of London, although there are times when it is easy to imagine you are on the coast because of the sound of lapping water against the hulls of boats and the gay, multi-coloured buildings around St Katharine's Dock.

The walk takes in part of the marvellous Silver Jubilee Walkway created in 1977 to commemorate the twenty-fifth anniversary of the Queen's accession to the throne. Although you are in the centre of London, the walkway steers you clear of the traffic but care should still be taken if you have young children with you. Our route includes the Tower of London, a trip across the Thames to HMS *Belfast* and of course Tower Bridge, probably the most famous bridge in the world.

Tower Bridge was built between 1886 and 1894 by Sir Horace Jones. It is a cantilever bridge with twin Gothic towers and a double-leaf bascule mechanism which opens to provide a 250 foot gap. It is a strange mix of drawbridge and suspension bridge. The two 1,000-ton bascules take 90 seconds to open to allow shipping to pass. It is still sometimes possible, by applying to the Guildhall, to get permission to be shown the bridge's engines. There used to be a pedestrian crossing along the upper walkway but this was closed to the public more than 50 years ago because it proved a favourite jumping spot for people wanting to take their own lives.

The opening times for Tower Bridge walk way are: April to October, 10am to 5.45pm; November to March, 10am to

TOWER BRIDGE

½ mile

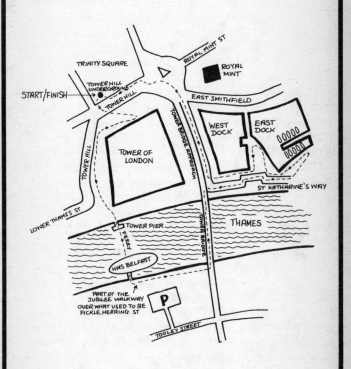

TRINITY SQUARE

ROYAL MINT ST

ROYAL MINT

TOWER HILL UNDERGROUND

START/FINISH

TOWER HILL

EAST SMITHFIELD

TOWER HILL

TOWER BRIDGE APPROACH

WEST DOCK

EAST DOCK

TOWER OF LONDON

ST KATHARINE'S WAY

LOWER THAMES ST

TOWER PIER

FERRY

TOWER BRIDGE

THAMES

HMS BELFAST

PART OF THE JUBILEE WALKWAY OVER WHAT USED TO BE PICKLE HERRING ST

P

TOOLEY STREET

- - ● - -	ROUTE
═══════	ROAD
P	PARKING

4pm. The bridge's museum, which houses one of the old engines, is open daily, 10am to 6.30pm. Visiting times for HMS *Belfast* are: March to October, Monday to Saturday, 9.30am to 5.45pm, Sunday 2pm to 5.45pm; November to February, Monday to Saturday, 9.30am to 4.30pm.

It is best to reach the start of the walk by taking a tube train to Tower Hill Underground station because during the week traffic is heavy and parking difficult. It is easier to park at weekends, but a journey in by tube on the District and Circle line all adds to the fun.

From the tube station in Trinity Square, head for the Tower of London along Tower Hill. Tower Hill was for more than 300 years the place where prisoners kept in the Tower were executed by beheading. 125 people lost their heads here, including Sir Thomas More, Thomas Cromwell and the Duke of Monmouth. The last execution took place there in 1747. At the top of Tower Hill close to the tube station you can still see part of the original city wall built by the Romans in the second century.

The Tower of London was started in 1078 by William the Conqueror at a point where the old Roman wall reached the river. The White Tower still retains its Norman chapel but is now surrounded by thirteenth-century walls. Throughout the centuries it was a garrison, armoury and royal palace. There was even a zoo there, founded in the fourteenth century, but the Victorians moved it. Cromwell abolished the palace, the Royal Mint moved out in 1810, and the observatory moved to Greenwich in 1675. The last prisoners were released in 1820, though before then many famous heads had been chopped off. Before their execution, many doomed prisoners carved their names into the stone walls of their cells in Bell Tower and St Thomas's Tower. Prisoners were often carried to the Tower by boat and entered through Traitor's Gate, which can be seen as you take the ferry across to the *Belfast*. In the Tower you will see the ravens, and legend has it that if they ever desert this home, disaster will befall Britain. Also to be seen are the famous Yeoman Guards, the Beefeaters; Queen's House, home of the Gov-

The Tower of London, still one of London's most popular attractions for visitors from all over the world

ernor; and the Jewel House. A visit to see the Crown Jewels is a must, and if you have a strong stomach you can visit the dungeons and torture chambers, mercifully now silent except for the plod and chatter of tourists.

A whole morning could be spent exploring the Tower but you should leave plenty of time to complete the walk because there is still much to see and do.

On leaving the Tower, walk down Tower Hill to the river and Tower Pier, where you can catch a ferry across to HMS *Belfast*. She was built in 1938 and was the largest cruiser in the Royal Navy at 11,000 tons. She played a back-up role in the Battle of the River Plate in 1939, and was at the Battle of North Cape in 1943 and the D-Day landings before becoming the flagship for the Fleet in the Far East. Her active career ended in 1963 and after a seven-year fight to save her, she opened as a floating museum in 1971. She is still in full working order and you can visit the operations room, mess decks, sick bay, galley and engine room.

Use the companionway to get to the south bank of the Thames, where you can join the Jubilee walk. This follows the route of a long-vanished street which used to be called Pickle Herring Street, although it never had anything to do with fish. It is thought to have been named after a sixteenth-century Dutch brewer who was known as Pickell Herring.

Follow the path eastwards for a hundred yards until you reach Tower Bridge. Cross over to the north bank of the Thames using the bridge and then walk up Tower Bridge Approach until it meets St Katharine's Way. Follow St Katharine's Way back down towards the river, pass the Tower Thistle Hotel to enter the docks and marina, and another world. You can spend hours strolling round the various features of the docks, or sit at one of the cafés.

St Katharine's Dock has a long history. There was a hospice there in 1146, founded by Queen Matilda, but it was in the nineteenth century that the various basins were excavated by Thomas Telford around warehouses and it became a destination for sailing ships from all corners of the world. The later large steamships could not use the docks so its popularity waned, but now the buildings have been carefully restored and as well as a modern marina, shops and restaurants, there is a fine collection of historic ships.

After visiting the dock head back towards St Katharine's Way, then northwards up Tower Bridge Approach before turning left into Tower Hill and heading back to the tube station.

Walk 3
TRINGFORD RESERVOIR HIDE
TRING, HERTS
2 miles

The Tring reservoirs are one of the most popular wildlife habitats in the south of England and attract birds throughout the year, so there is usually lots to see in any season. There you will find many different species of nesting birds in the spring as well as migrants which pop in to rest and feed before continuing their spring and autumn journeys. The reservoirs are also popular as a wintering base for thousands of birds.

This is therefore a good place to visit if you are interested in birdwatching, or thinking about taking it up. Flocks of ducks up to a thousand strong can be viewed with ease during the winter months, including many rare species such as goosander, ring-necked and ferruginous duck. Up to 15,000 gulls roost at Wilstone reservoir and many species of wader, including rarities, can be spotted on the mudbanks in the spring and autumn. The Tringford hide is particularly good for waders, including unusual visitors such as the avocet and spoonbill. The little ringed plover first nested here in 1938, the first recorded nesting site in the UK. There is also an interesting heronry where the birds have made their homes in the reed beds rather than trees, their usual preferred site.

The reservoirs were built between 1802 and 1839 to store water for the Grand Union Canal which runs from Birmingham to London. They are about 400 feet above sea level and are fed by natural springs. They are known as marl lakes, a type found only in limestone and chalk areas. The waters are rich in minerals which support large fish and plant populations,

TRINGFORD RESERVOIR HIDE

½ mile

TO DUNSTABLE

ANGLER'S RETREAT
PUBLIC
HOUSE

START/FINISH

P

GRAND UNION CANAL

STARTOP'S
END

STARTOP'S END
RESERVOIR

MARSWORTH
RESERVOIR

AYLESBURY,
WILSTONE
RESERVOIR
+ A41

A41 TRING + LONDON

TRINGFORD
RESERVOIR

HIDE

TRINGFORD
PUMPING
STATION

- - -	ROUTE
═══	ROAD
⊢—⊣	GATE OR STILE
⊥	LOCK
⊨	BRIDGE

N

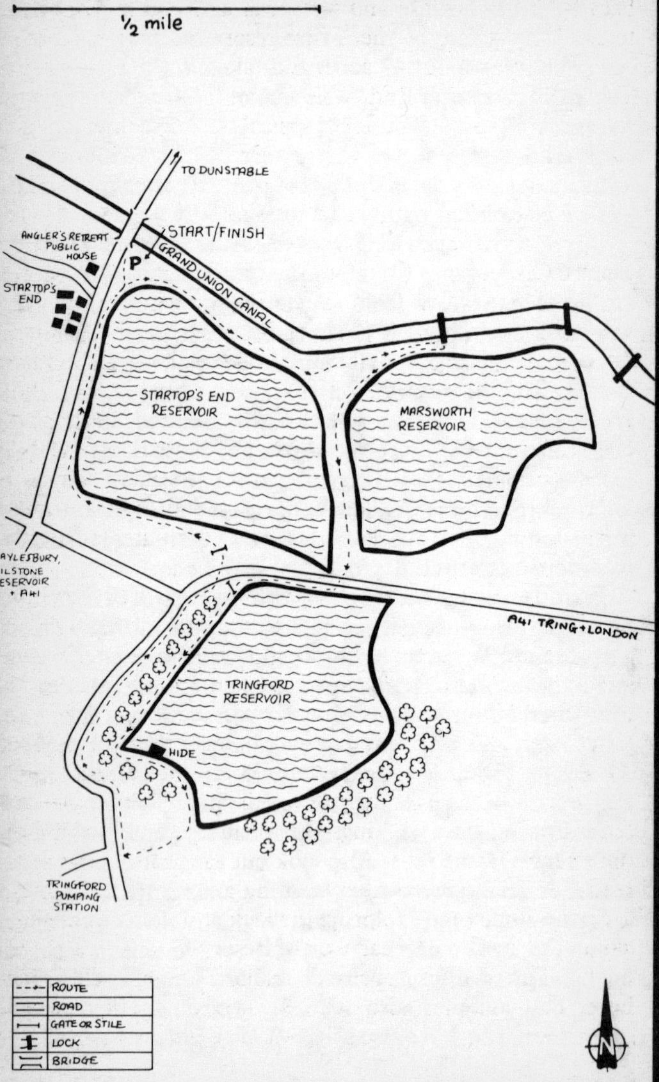

and it is these which attract and support the birdlife.

The area was designated a national nature reserve in 1955 because of its birdlife and botanical and entomological interest. The whole of the Tring reservoirs national nature reserve covers about 47 acres and takes in the reservoirs of Tringford, Startop's End, Wilstone and Marsworth. Because the area is an important site of special scientific interest and a national nature reserve, visitors are asked to follow three simple rules – not to pick plants or disturb animals and birds, to stay on marked paths, and to take litter home.

Our route follows a well-marked nature trail laid out by the Nature Conservancy Council. The walk can be just a pleasant afternoon's stroll, or form the basis for a whole day's bird-watching expedition. A useful guide to the trail is available from the Nature Conservancy Council, Northminster House, Peterborough PE1 1UA. The walking is easy, there are no hills and the path is very clearly marked. Perhaps the only difficult part is actually finding the car park off the B489 just before the Grand Union Canal. The easiest way is to approach on the A41 from either Tring or Aylesbury and then turn north on the B489 to the car park across the road from the Angler's Retreat public house.

The first section takes you along the towpath of the Grand Union Canal to the first of six locks that form the Tring Steps, a clever piece of engineering which lifts the canal almost 400 feet. Every time a boat wants to go through the lock, over 50,000 gallons of water are needed to adjust the canal level, and when the gates are opened this water is lost. That is why the reservoirs were built. In the summer swifts and swallows dart over the path, while in the winter you may see yellow wagtails or kingfishers, which come down from the streams in the hills. Also look out for bearded tits in the reeds, or great grey shrikes hunting among the brambles.

Spend some time exploring the lock and then double back along the banks of Marsworth Reservoir and watch the ducks. Tufted duck, pochard, mallard and shoveler breed here, but you may also see teal, wigeon, goldeneye and goosander. There are also grebes and geese, grey herons and

A grey heron, one of the many birds to be spotted from the hide at Tringford Reservoir

the secretive bittern, which often winters here.

Bear to the left, between Marsworth Reservoir on your left and Startop's End Reservoir on your right. This stretch of path between the two reservoirs is popular with anglers and the waters are well stocked with roach, bream, tench, perch and pike. The magnificent great crested grebe is a common sight now on the waters although only a century ago it had been almost hunted to extinction for its feathers. Spring is the time to visit to watch its incredible courtship displays.

Towards the top end of the reservoirs, before the path crosses the A41, you are close to the heronry in the reeds and from December to June you can watch the birds with ease. The reed birds here also provide the home for a colony of reed warblers which annually makes the 7,500-mile trip from Africa to summer at Tring. The scrubland and reed beds are ideal for warblers and you can spot half a dozen different species or more, such as chiffchaff, sedge warbler, blackcap, willow warbler and lesser whitethroat. They are all beautiful singers and compete for air space during the summer.

When you reach the A41, turn right and follow the road for a short way until you reach the stile which gives access to the bank of Tringford Reservoir. There are always plenty of ducks to be seen and many interesting plants along the path, such as water mint, gypsywort, meadowsweet and skullcap.

As you follow the bank of Tringford Reservoir on your left, the path takes you through a small area of trees where you might hear or even see woodpeckers. The trees are old and dying and attract many curious fungi, including Jew's Ear which can be seen all year round. Here you will also see just how ravaging Dutch Elm disease has been, but already other species are competing to take over the wood.

The path swings sharply to the left and leads you to the hide which is the object of your walk.

When the time comes to leave, continue on the path, which passes a pumping station and cottage on the left. Here you turn right onto a metalled road which after about 500 yards brings you down to the A41. Turn right, then left over a stile to Startop's End Reservoir. The path bears right to follow the reservoir back, along which many birds can be spotted as well as many unusual marshland plants – round-fruited rush, orange foxtail and mudwort. On the corner where the path turns right to follow the bank, you can also see the pollarded black poplar, a native English tree but now becoming rare.

You are now nearing the end of the walk. There is a pillbox built during the last war just in case the Germans tried to invade by flying boats, but it and the walls of the reservoir are now being taken over by vegetation, as nature again takes control.

Walk 4
IVINGHOE BEACON
BUCKINGHAMSHIRE
6 miles

Ivinghoe Beacon gives some of the finest views to be seen in the whole of southern England. The Beacon itself marks one end of the Ridgeway long-distance footpath; the National Trust car park attracts visitors who do not want to walk quite so far.

From the top, nearly 800 feet above sea level, there are spectacular views in every direction. To the south and east, much of the land belongs to the National Trust; and you can look out to Moneybury Hill and the monument to the 3rd Earl of Bridgewater, famous as one of the great canal pioneers of the eighteenth century. To the east you can see the white lion cut into hillside chalk near Whipsnade and, to the north, the village of Edlesborough. You can also look out to the south-west and see the roads which follow the routes of the Upper and Lower Icknield Way, two of the oldest prehistoric trackways in Britain, which unite at Ivinghoe.

The Beacon is popular with radio-controlled model plane enthusiasts and hang gliders. You can see the remnants of an Iron Age contour fort, at least 2,500 years old. With such views for miles in every direction, you can appreciate its defensive position, and see why beacons lit there could be spotted throughout the surrounding countryside.

As well as a very pleasant walk (though a little steep in places), there is lots to see in the area, especially the many National Trust properties. Much of the land here is run by the Trust, including The Coombe, Crawley Wood, Ringshall

IVINGHOE BEACON

1 mile

CHILTERN FARM

COLLYER'S HOUSE

DAGNALL FARM

DAGNALL

A4146

B4506

RADIO STATION

WARD'S COOMBE

GALLOWS HILL

WARD'S HURST FARM

HANGING COOMBE

ALTERNATIVE ROUTE BESIDE ROAD IF YOU DO NOT WANT TO CROSS FIELDS

COOMBE HOLE

IVINGHOE BEACON

P

START/FINISH

P

DRIVE HOUSE

CLIPPER DOWN

STEPS HILL

INCOMBE HOLE

MINOR ROAD

RIDGEWAY

B488

IVINGHOE

WINDMILL

B488

B488

→→→	ROUTE
══	ROAD
I——I	GATE OR STILE
P	PARKING

Coppice and Dockey Wood – all of which you pass on the walk. The Beacon is also owned by the Trust.

Before you set off on your walk, however, visit the village of Ivinghoe which gave its name to the hero Ivanhoe in Sir Walter Scott's novel. There is a fine inn, the King's Head, originally built in the thirteenth century and rebuilt two hundred years later. The church, dedicated to St Mary the Virgin, dates from the thirteenth century, although it has seen a great deal of alteration. It has a marvellous roof with the outstretched wings of angels reaching up into the timbers, and stone statues of both people and animals. The agricultural tradition of the village is reflected in the church: the timbers are decorated with carved flowers, and there are roses and leaves carved into the timber in the chancel. The pulpit is Jacobean and the lectern dates from Elizabethan times. Examine the ends of the pews and look carefully at the carved poppy heads – inside you will see twisted faces, typical of this sort of medieval work.

You can also visit Pitstone Windmill (National Trust) which is about half a mile to the south of the village. It is one of the oldest post mills in Britain. Built in 1627, it has been restored to working order by the Chiltern Society.

You reach the clearly signposted car parks below the Beacon by following the B489. This travels south-west from Dunstable, or north-east after branching off from the A41(T) Tring to Aylesbury Road. If you are travelling south from Leighton Buzzard, take the B488 and turn left onto the B489 at Ivinghoe village.

The walk starts from the car park to the south of the Beacon. Turn left and follow the road for a short distance until you reach the first entrance on the right leading to a gravel path. Climb the rutted, often muddy slope and at the top you emerge from the scrub and meet the Ridgeway path. As you climb the slope on your right is Steps Hill and the famous Incombe Hole, which has a depth of 250 feet. The Chiltern Society, which has done so much to protect the area, was responsible for clearing the low-lying bushes from the slopes of the combe, thus revealing it in all its glory.

Pitstone Windmill, one of the many sights to be spotted from the top of Ivinghoe Beacon

Follow the Ridgeway path for a short way, over one stile and then down hill. Just before reaching a second stile, turn left along the fence until you come to yet another stile which takes you into the wood on your left. Cross over the interchange of footpaths but at the second turn right and climb to the top of Clipper Down. From here you can look north to Ivinghoe Beacon and north-west to the windmill with the village of Ivinghoe behind.

Follow the path, which now leads down towards the road, and go left at a fork. Take another left-hand turn onto a well-worn track; this takes you to the road. Turn right for a very short distance along the road and then cross it to walk up the drive to Ward's Hurst Farm. The footpath skirts to the left of the farm and crosses the farmyard to continue as a well-marked path straight ahead. The trees on your left are part of the valley known as Hanging Coombe.

The footpath continues ahead and downhill and you should keep the fence on your right. The path then hugs the right-hand boundary of a finger of trees pointing down into the valley. Apart from a wiggle as you veer past the farm, this section of the walk – from the last road to where you join another road just north of Dagnall – is virtually a straight line.

Walk to the left of Hog Hall and onto the drive; this takes you to the A4146 just beyond Dagnall Farm.

Turn left and follow the road past Collyers House and Chiltern Farm on your right, until you come to a massive radio station complex. On the left-hand side of the road, just beyond the farm (on the other side of the road) take the bridleway which follows the fence beside the radio station. It runs between the fence and the private road to Ward's Coombe.

The path follows very straight lines as it goes along by the fence of the radio station. Keep following the radio station fence, keeping it on your right, until you come to the corner of the field. The next two fields are crossed by rights of way but may be obstructed by crops, in which case skirt round the field, making your way to the summit of Gallows Hill and then continuing uphill to the Beacon itself. If you do not want to skirt the fields, you can make your way onto the B489 and follow the road for some distance before turning left again on the footpath which takes you to the summit of Ivinghoe Beacon. It is easy, however, to follow the 'new' path round the sides of the fields. There is a gate to be crossed if you stick to the footpath from Gallows Hill, which has been reported wired up in the past. It is across the footpath and can be climbed but there is also a stile now.

From the top of the Beacon retrace the final steps of the Ridgeway Path back downhill towards the road, and then follow this back to the car park.

Walk 5
WEST WYCOMBE CAVES
BUCKINGHAMSHIRE
4 miles

This is another of my favourite walks because it is simple to follow and there is lots to see. As well as the very attractive village of West Wycombe, there is West Wycombe House, now owned by the National Trust, and the famous caves, former home of the infamous Hell Fire Club.

Although you have to pay to visit both these attractions, they are well worth it and together with the walk itself can make up a very enjoyable day.

The Hell Fire Club, formed in 1746, held its secret meetings deep inside the caves. There are rumours of wild orgies and devil worship, but most of the activities of the club are still shrouded in mystery. Local stories are quite clear on one thing, though: this is where the 'Wycombe wenches left their last memories of their innocence'! The quarter of a mile long caves at their lowest depth are 300 feet below ground, and at the bottom level there is the 'Inner Temple' where members of the club used to meet. Water runs through the lowest galleries of the caves and it is said that the club members used a boat to ferry themselves to their inner sanctum. Today's visitors cross by a bridge.

The caves were originally excavated to obtain chalk for local road building before they became notorious as the location for meetings of the Hell Fire Club. Both the caves and West Wycombe House opposite are linked with the Dashwood family, who have been in the village for the last 250 years. The village itself is fascinating because it is owned

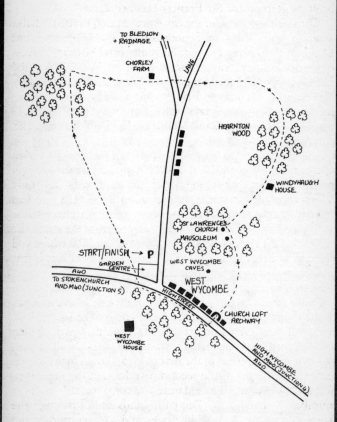

WEST WYCOMBE CAVES

1 mile

TO BLEDLOW + RADNAGE

CHORLEY FARM

LANE

HEARNTON WOOD

WINDYHAUGH HOUSE

ST LAWRENCES CHURCH
MAUSOLEUM

START/FINISH → P

GARDEN CENTRE

WEST WYCOMBE CAVES

A40
TO STOKENCHURCH AND M40 (JUNCTION 5)

WEST WYCOMBE

HIGH STREET

CHURCH LOFT ARCHWAY

WEST WYCOMBE HOUSE

HIGH WYCOMBE AND M40 (JUNCTION 4)
A40

- - - -	ROUTE
———	ROAD
P	PARKING

N

entirely by the National Trust. The whole village was bought by the Royal Society of Arts in the late 1920s and then transferred to the Trust.

West Wycombe House is open to the public during the summer. The house is Palladian, influenced by Adam, and built by Repton for Sir Francis Dashwood.

The opening times for the caves are: March to April, daily, 1pm to 6pm; May to September, daily, 11am to 6pm; October, daily, 1pm to 6pm; November to February, Saturday and Sunday only, 12noon to 4pm. West Wycombe House is open: June, Monday to Friday, 2pm to 6pm; July and August, Monday to Friday, and Sunday, 2pm to 6pm; guided tours on weekdays only. The house's grounds are open: Easter, Spring Bank Holiday, May Day, Sundays and Mondays, 2pm to 6pm.

You reach West Wycombe – which lies on the A40 – from the north on the A4010 or A4128. On the former you will come to West Wycombe first; the signposts say only 'Wycombe'. If you are travelling in on the A4128 you will have to go into High Wycombe before turning right onto the A40 which will take you into the village. From the south the village is best approached on the A404 or the M40 where you can exit at either junction 4 or 5. Parking in the village is free and there is a large park, clearly signposted, next to a large garden centre.

Walk from the car park to turn right on the main road. Follow this for a short distance until you see the footpath on your right in the corner of a field. Take this path, which crosses the fields diagonally towards the trees ahead of you. Cross a stile at the end of the first field, and then make for the gate in the corner of the second. Go through the gate, turn left and skirt round the field until you come to a stile with the number '5' fixed to it. The path winds uphill through the trees. The walk is steep in places and can be muddy and slippery, but it is easy to follow throughout because it has been waymarked by members of the Chiltern Society who have painted prominent white arrows on fences, stiles and trees to make it perfectly clear which route to follow.

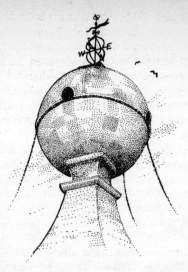

The golden ball gracing the top of St Lawrence's Church, from where the Hell Fire Club used to look out over the surrounding countryside

A lot of the walk is through woodland which is owned by local estates where shooting is popular. Gamekeepers patrol the woods, in which are bred partridge and pheasant, so dogs must be kept on leads. There are constant reminders that the land on either side of the path is private, so do not stray. There are ample signs of deer living in these woods, and you will see trees stripped of their bark.

Towards the brow of the hill, still in the trees, the path runs into a much broader one. Turn right, and follow this path as it veers to the right, over the summit and then down the hill towards Chorley Farm. The footpath is still clearly marked and runs to the right of the farm. Cross the road and go through the gate ahead of you numbered '12'. Walk straight ahead, keeping to the footpath which runs alongside the fence, to a lane at the end. Horses are sometimes kept in these fields and they can be a bit frisky, so take care.

Cross the lane to a stile, go over this and follow the path

uphill. The path can be a bit slippery after rain. Head for the trees and a gate marked '13'. Follow the white arrows through the trees until the path joins another. Take the path on the right with the waymark arrow on the left of you. This path takes you through very old woodland, Hearnton Wood, before emerging out of the trees near Windyhaugh House. The path runs to the right of the house, parallel to the lane, then veering to the right and through some gates to enter the churchyard of St. Lawrence's.

For much of the walk, once out of the trees, you should have been able to spot the golden ball that tops the church. The ball is hollow and inside there is seating for ten people. The inspiration for the ball is said to have come from the churches of Moscow and Venice.

Next door to the church is the splendid Mausoleum built in 1763 by Sir Francis Dashwood, who was enormously influential and was for a time chancellor of the Exchequer. He decreed in his will that his heart be removed and kept in a marble urn in one of the recesses of the Mausoleum, and he left 50 guineas for purchase of the urn. Apparently his wishes were carried out, but the urn was stolen some years later.

The caves are just down the hill from the Mausoleum. After visiting them, make your way down the footpath to the village. Many of the timbered houses are 400 years old or more, and of particular interest is Church Loft House. You have to pass under its archway as you descend the hill from the caves, and in the house you can still see the old prison where malefactors were held as well as the chain where they were strung up for whipping.

Turn right into the High Street for the short walk back to the car park.

Walk 6
KEW GARDENS
LONDON
2¾ miles

Kew Gardens, or the Royal Botanic Gardens as they are officially known, are the world's most famous. For decades the Gardens were a favourite country residence of royalty and it was Augusta, mother of George III, who in 1759 had a formal garden laid out, covering nine acres.

The Gardens expanded and acquired plants and trees from all over the world. In 1841 the Gardens were donated to the nation, although Queen Victoria still had her own private park alongside. In 1898 she donated this to the nation as well, and by 1904 Kew Gardens had expanded to 300 acres and was already internationally famous both as a seat of scientific study and as a place of public enjoyment.

The gardens contain plants from every corner of the globe, including many species which have become extinct in their native countries. The western half of the gardens is devoted mostly to trees and the arboretum, while the eastern half is occupied by lawns, flower beds and the massive glasshouses, some of the largest in the world, which are all slowly being modernised. Each of the glasshouses is devoted to a particular region of the world and the conditions inside match them perfectly. There are tropical houses, alpine houses, and so on.

Apart from the glasshouses, including one built by Decimus Burton in the 1840s, the Chinese Pagoda is a famous landmark. It has ten storeys and is 163 feet high and octagonal in shape.

KEW GARDENS

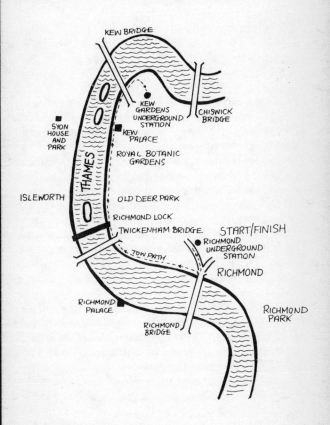

KEW BRIDGE

KEW GARDENS UNDERGROUND STATION

CHISWICK BRIDGE

SYON HOUSE AND PARK

KEW PALACE

THAMES

ROYAL BOTANIC GARDENS

ISLEWORTH

OLD DEER PARK

RICHMOND LOCK

TWICKENHAM BRIDGE

START/FINISH

RICHMOND UNDERGROUND STATION

TOW PATH

RICHMOND

RICHMOND PARK

RICHMOND PALACE

RICHMOND BRIDGE

1 mile

- - - ROUTE
═══ BRIDGE
── ROAD

N

There is also a 225-foot flagpole on Victory Hill, made from a single Douglas Fir. It was felled in British Columbia in 1959 when it was thought to be at least 370 years old.

There are two museums housed at Kew; a general plant museum containing tens of thousands of specimens gathered over the last 100 years, and a wood museum. Other buildings of note are the Dutch House, now known as Kew Palace, the Queen's Cottage and the Orangery. The Dutch House was built in 1631 and was used by the Royal Family until 1818. It is still open to the public and has been preserved as it was when used by George III and his family.

The Gardens themselves involve quite a lot of walking, so this is a fairly short walk. It also takes advantage of the easy availability of public transport in London. The walk is invigorating and it does prove that even though you are only a few miles from the heart of London, it is still possible to capture some of the peace and tranquillity of the countryside whilst surrounded by one of the largest cities in the world.

The walk route, which is flat and on well-made paths, is part of what is likely to become designated as a long-distance footpath running from Putney for more than 150 miles to the source of the Thames in the springs of the Cotswolds. Although official blessing for the scheme has been given, after many years of persuasion from the Ramblers' Association, it is likely to be some years still before it becomes a reality.

There are only two slight drawbacks with the walk. Because the river is tidal parts of the towpath may be flooded during very high tides. This happens occasionally, but it is always possible to duck inland for a few yards down one of the many lanes to bypass the problem.

Park in Richmond, bearing in mind that you will be coming back to the Underground station there. Plenty of off-street parks, and meters, mean that parking is no problem, especially at weekends. Join the river towpath at Richmond Bridge, and turn right. Follow the path under Twickenham Bridge and past Richmond Lock. From here there are wonderful views of Regency Richmond. On your bank of the

The Hammersmith suspension bridge, one of the many splendid bridges spanning the Thames, is passed on the extension to the Kew Gardens walk

river you pass Old Deer Park, home of London Welsh Rugby Club, while on the opposite bank is Isleworth, then Syon Park.

Syon House was first a monastery and then a convent until the dissolution of the monasteries under Henry VIII. The house became the property of the Earl of Northumberland during the reign of James I, and it is still the home of the present Duke. The family crest features a lion and a huge stone effigy of that animal dominates the roof. The lion used to stand guard at Northumberland House, the London home of the Dukes, just off the Strand. This property was demolished in the last century, but the lion was saved and transferred to Syon House.

Just before Kew Bridge you arrive at your objective, the Botanic Gardens. There is an entrance close to the towpath.

The 'village' of Kew is also worth exploring. Kew has been the home of many celebrities such as Archbishop Lang, Gainsborough and the painter Zoffany, famous for his 'Last Supper', who lived here for 30 years until 1810. Gainsborough and Zoffany are buried in the parish church of St Anne.

From Kew Gardens Underground station, take a west-bound District Line train the one stop back to Richmond. Richmond itself is well worth exploring. Little remains of the palace built by Henry VII, apart from the gateway, but by calling it Richmond after his Yorkshire earldom, he obliged the locals to change the name of the village from West Sheen, and so the name lives on. It was popular with royalty for many generations, and here Elizabeth I died. Maids in Honour Row was built in 1724 on the Green to accommodate the ladies in waiting on the Princess of Wales who resided at Richmond Lodge (also unfortunately gone) in the Old Deer Park. There are many more fine houses to see if you have time.

If you prefer a long walk, instead of heading for the Underground station when you leave Kew Gardens, return to the towpath and continue on towards Putney. You will find yourself walking the Boat Race course in reverse, passing Mortlake, Barnes Bridge, Hammersmith Bridge and, on the opposite bank, Fulham Palace. This extension is approximately 2¾ miles and at the end of it is Putney Bridge Underground station from which a train may be taken (change at Earl's Court) back to Richmond.

Walk 7
BROADWOOD'S TOWER
BOX HILL, SURREY
3½ miles

Broadwood's Tower is a round building of flint stone, with no door. It was built by Thomas Broadwood, a piano manufacturer, who purchased nearby Juniper Hall in 1814. No-one knows whether the tower was built as a folly or if it had a more sensible purpose, to be used as a signalling tower, for instance. Some people suggest it was built to commemorate the British victory at Waterloo in 1815. Just before the tower on our chosen route, a grassy vantage point makes an ideal place for a picnic or some birdwatching.

Box Hill is one of the most famous beauty spots in the south of England and attracts tens of thousands of visitors every year. Almost all the land is owned by the National Trust and it is criss-crossed by footpaths that are all waymarked, so there is plenty of walking. The huge mass of Box Hill rises to nearly 700 feet above sea level and has always been a favourite visiting place for locals and strangers alike. Jane Austen used the grassy slopes as the spot where her characters picnicked in her novel *Emma*, although I hope that your day ends more harmoniously than theirs. Most people come here because it is the highest point in the south-east of England and on a clear day you can see the Crowborough radio beacon on Ashdown Forest 24 miles away and Shoreham Gap, a little further to the west and 26 miles away.

Although the area attracts many visitors, most are content to sit in their cars or to walk the few steps to the observation

BROADWOOD'S TOWER

½ mile

TO MICKLEHAM

MINOR ROAD

JUNIPER HALL FIELD STUDIES CENTRE

BROADWOOD'S TOWER

LODGE HILL

JUNIPER BOTTOM

MINOR ROAD

A24

P

RIVER MOLE

ZIG ZAG ROAD

TO STATION

A24

P

ZIG ZAG VALLEY

TO DORKING

X THREE BEECH TREES

RESTAURANT CAFE

NATIONAL TRUST INFORMATION CENTRE

START/FINISH

P

DONKEY GREEN

SWISS COTTAGE

P

BOX HILL VILLAGE

OBSERVATION POINT (SALOMON'S MEMORIAL)

-·-→	ROUTE
	ROAD
〰〰	RIVER
P	PARKING

N

post. The walks themselves, although popular, are rarely crowded and in the autumn and winter you can often have them to yourself. The walks are easy but they do encounter some reasonably steep gradients, and in a couple of places there are quite steep flights of wooden steps which need care. Young children can find themselves accelerating uncontrollably down them if you are not careful. Much of the route is also used as a bridleway and this can lead to the path being churned up by horses' hooves, so wellington boots or good sturdy walking boots are essential. The area is so rich in wildlife that a good pair of binoculars will enable you to enjoy the walk all the more. In fact, because it has so much to offer, allow two hours or more to complete the walk.

Box Hill is best reached from the south by taking the B2032 Headley road from the roundabout on the A25 Reigate to Dorking road. The road climbs steeply uphill past Buckland Station and you must turn left, still heading for Headley, and then turn again to the left following the signpost to Box Hill village. A short way past the village you will have to cross a number of 'sleeping policemen' before reaching the National Trust's Information Centre. There is a restaurant and snack bar next door and a number of parking areas.

From the north it is best to drive down the A24 through Leatherhead and then turn off to the left on the B2209 Mickelham road before turning into the National Trust's zig-zag road which takes you to the Information Centre and observation point. The observation point is also a memorial to Leopold Salmon of Norbury Park, who gave the land to the Trust in 1914.

The observation post makes the ideal starting-point for our walk, which follows trails created by the National Trust through spectacular woodland scenery. Park your car in the NT parking area across the road from the Information Centre. Walk across the open grassland, and over another bend of the road to reach the observation post. Here you can enjoy a 180-degree panorama, with the most breathtaking views on a clear day. When we arrived to do the walk, we were actually above the clouds which were hanging in the

A tomb in the woods on Box Hill, one of the many curiosities to be discovered

valley below us. When we finished and returned to the spot again, the clouds had gone, the sun was shining and we could see for miles.

From the observation post head westwards, following the red waymark signs. You go past Swiss Cottage, where James Logie Baird carried out some of his early experiments, and then follow the red waymark signs into the wood. You pass several magnificent yews and a number of the box trees which give their name to the area.

At the no.3 red waymark sign you will see a stone marking the site where Major Peter Labelliere was buried head down so that he would be the right way up at the end of the 'topsy turvy world'.

The path then emerges into a long grassy slope with fine

views on all sides; you can see the Burford Bridge Hotel in the valley on your left. Sheep are still allowed to graze the hill slopes to prevent trees encroaching.

The path in places follows a line of exposed chalk and this can be quite sticky underfoot. By the no.7 red waymark sign turn right and go down the first of two sets of wooden steps taking you into the Zig Zag Valley. The second flight has 118 steps and, while secure, should be taken carefully.

At the bottom turn right to follow the Zig Zag Road for a short distance and then head off up the valley, following the red waymark sign into the woods. This is quite a long uphill climb but there are lots of good excuses for stopping to inspect things and get your breath back. You will certainly see grey squirrels darting among the trees and may be lucky enough to see the much more timid roe deer.

The path crosses Zig Zag Road nearly at the top of the hill and almost immediately reaches a stand of three magnificent beech trees. Go to the left of these trees for about fifty yards and you will join a well-worn trail with grey waymark signs. Turn left and keep following the grey arrows until you emerge from the trees to look out over Zig Zag Valley. Here is the grassy area already mentioned and, shortly afterwards, Broadwood's Tower itself.

When you are rested, follow the path as it winds its way down through marvellous woodland to emerge at a spot overlooking Juniper Bottom. Here another flight of wooden steps helps you make the descent to the valley floor.

But having come down, you know you must go back up again, so turn right and follow the path back into the woods of box trees and yew. The path climbs steadily uphill and can be a bit tacky underfoot but eventually it ends at Donkey Green, just a short distance from the obervation post where you started. The Green gets its name because when the railway brought the first day visitors in 1867, the children used to take donkey-rides here.

This is not a long walk but there is lots to see and the views are spectacular. This chalk escarpment which forms part of the North Downs makes an ideal spot for a family outing.

Walk 8
ALLINGTON CASTLE
NEAR MAIDSTONE, KENT
2 miles, with 3 mile optional detour

Allington Castle has been a Carmelite retreat since 1951 and stands beside the River Medway in beautiful gardens. It is a thirteenth-century fortified manor house, with thick walls and battlements. In the fifteenth century it was bought and restored by the Wyatt family, who added the Long Gallery. The castle fell into disrepair with the death of Sir Thomas Wyatt, executed in 1554 for leading a Kentish revolt against Queen Mary. The castle was bought by Lord Conway at the beginning of this century and restored. Although it is now used as a retreat, it is open daily in the afternoons from 2pm to 4pm (except Christmas Day) and there are guided tours when demand is sufficient. The grounds are open to the public free of charge.

This is a good, easy walk to introduce the town-dweller to the countryside because there is something to interest every member of the family. As well as the castle, the walk can be extended to include a nature trail, an exhibition of the county's long agricultural history, a river walk and a working lock. Nowhere is the walk difficult, although there is a small hill to climb.

The walk starts at the car park at Cobtree Manor Park, which is to be found off the Forstal Road between the Running Horse roundabout and Aylesford village. If you are travelling on the M20, leave at junction 6 and follow the signs to Maidstone until you arrive at the roundabout after about half a mile. Ignore the A229 to Maidstone and continue

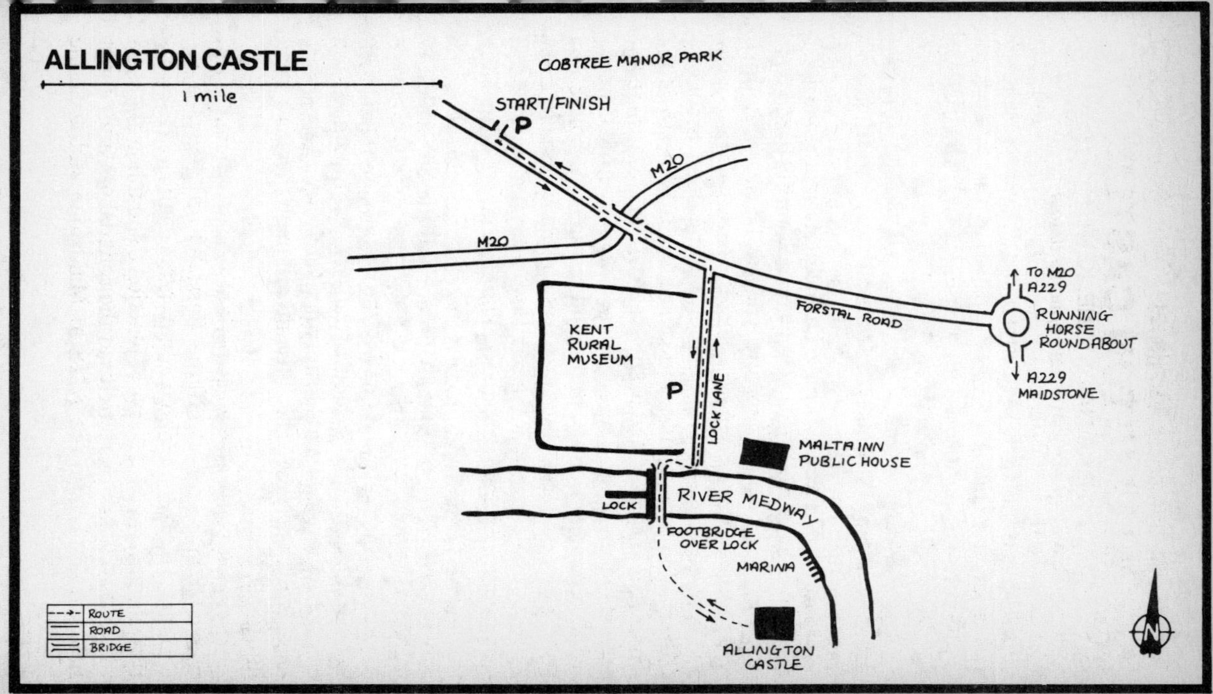

ALLINGTON CASTLE

1 mile

COBTREE MANOR PARK

START/FINISH

P

M20

M20

RUNNING HORSE ROUNDABOUT

TO M20 A229

A229 MAIDSTONE

FORSTAL ROAD

LOCK LANE

P

KENT RURAL MUSEUM

MALTA INN PUBLIC HOUSE

RIVER MEDWAY

LOCK

FOOTBRIDGE OVER LOCK

MARINA

ALLINGTON CASTLE

N

←·→	ROUTE
---	ROAD
	BRIDGE

round until you see the Forstal Road turn-off for Aylesford. Cobtree Manor Park is almost half a mile down the Forstal Road, on the right just after a bridge crossing the busy M20 motorway.

To start, walk back down Forstal Road towards the Running Horse roundabout, and after about 300 yards, turn right down Lock Lane. This is signposted to the Kent Rural Museum, which you pass on your right and which is well worth a visit; it is open daily.

The museum covers 27 acres of land next to Allington Lock and depicts Kent's agricultural story, both past and present, through the use of exhibits, buildings, machinery and livestock. There is a fine farmyard pond with an area of osiers – traditionally grown for thatching – planted at one end. There are oast-houses, showing the history and cultivation of hops for brewing, and a small hop garden. In the outbuildings there is a fine collection of agricultural machinery, as well as dairy and harvesting equipment. Other features include arable plots, an orchard and an apiary. A new feature is a hamlet built to show bygone village life and featuring many rural crafts now threatened with extinction.

After visiting the museum head on down Lock Lane for the River Medway and Allington Lock. This is the first lock to be met by vessels coming up from the Swale, the estuary where the Thames and Medway meet. The river is about 150 yards away from the Rural Museum and there is a pleasant pub.

You can spend some time here walking along the towpath or helping the lock-keeper open the gates, because this is still a very busy stretch of water, although mostly used now by pleasure craft.

Cross over the river and follow the clearly marked signs to Allington Castle, which is about three-quarters of a mile away, along a quiet, tree-lined lane.

This is an 'out-and-back' walk rather than a circular one, so after enjoying the castle and its grounds, retrace your steps back across the river and past the Rural Museum – an ideal opportunity to visit it if you did not do so on the way to the

One of the many exhibits at the Kent Rural Museum

castle. Walk up Lock Lane, turn left into Forstal Road and so back to the car.

If you have the time and are still feeling energetic, there is a nature trail through Cobtree Manor Park (just over one mile long), or you can walk right round the perimeter of the park (just under three miles). A guide to the nature trail, pointing out things of interest along the way, can be sought from the warden. If you prefer the extended route round the edge of the park, follow the signs which take you through a public golf-course.

Cobtree Manor (now a private property) used to be known as Coptray Friars and belonged to Aylesford Priory, in the nearby village, half a mile to the west on the banks of the Medway. It was famed during the last century for its Pickwickian Parties, and the lake is supposed to have been Charles Dickens's source of inspiration for Dingley Dell. When the Manor was the home of Sir Garrard and Lady Edna Tyrwhitt-Drake, the surrounding parkland was turned into a zoo and opened to the public in 1933. At that time it had the

45

largest collection of wild animals in any Commonwealth zoo. When Sir Garrard died in 1964, he bequeathed the park, including the golf-course 'for the benefit of the inhabitants of Maidstone and other members of the public'.

The park now consists of the clearly marked circular nature trail with its many vantage points over the historic village of Aylesford and neighbouring farmland. The trail takes you through marvellous woodland but there are many other things to see. I have seen foxes here, and there are signs of badgers. The wide estuary of the Medway is a natural route for many birds, and the woods are rich in wildlife. It is possible to see the junction of the Gault Clay and the Folkestone Sands which have been exposed by the River Medway. The footpath is very easy to follow through the woods, and every so often there are spurs off the main path, taking you up to a vantage point. One of the first of these allows you to overlook Aylesford, one of the oldest villages in Kent. The medieval bridge and houses clustered on the northern bank of the Medway have not changed for 500 years. This was the setting for the Battle of Aylesford, when Hengist and Horsa defeated the Britons in 455 AD. Horsa was slain but Hengist became King of Kent for the next 33 years.

The walk also takes you through several different types of vegetation with a wide selection of wild flowers to be identified, including the interesting Stinking Iris, so named because of the terrible smell given off by the plant's leaves when crushed. The different vegetations also support many species of butterflies and more than a dozen different ones can be spotted.

The longer walk round the edge of the park takes you past the Elephant House, the last relic of the zoo which was disbanded at the outbreak of the Second World War.

Walk 9
PENSHURST PLACE
KENT
5 miles

This is one of my favourite family walks because it is not too arduous, takes in one of Kent's prettiest villages and has as its objective one of the finest stately homes in the land. There are also lovely paths to follow through parkland and woodland and along the banks of the graceful River Medway.

The beautiful old village of Penshurst lies on the B2176 to the west of Tonbridge and Tunbridge Wells. To the north is the village of Chiddingstone with its castle and a little further west is Hever, also with a magnificent castle. So if you are keen on visiting castles there is ample to keep you busy all day in this one small area.

The village gets its name from the Saxon word 'hurst' for a settlement in the woods. Sir Stephen de Penchester was Lord of the Manor during the reign of Edward I, and 'Penchester's hurst' became abridged to Penshurst. Sir Stephen was also Lord Warden of the Cinque Ports. In 1338 the estate was bought by a City of London merchant, Sir John de Pulteney. He was Lord Mayor of London four times and built the first manor house, parts of which still remain today. The house and estate then passed through many owners, including the Dukes of Bedford and Gloucester, brothers of Henry V. In 1552, the estate was granted to Sir William Sidney by Edward VI and Penshurst Place was created. The house has been in the hands of the Sidney family ever since.

Today, the Place incorporates the great hall, solar and buttery built by Pulteney around 1340. The hall is the finest

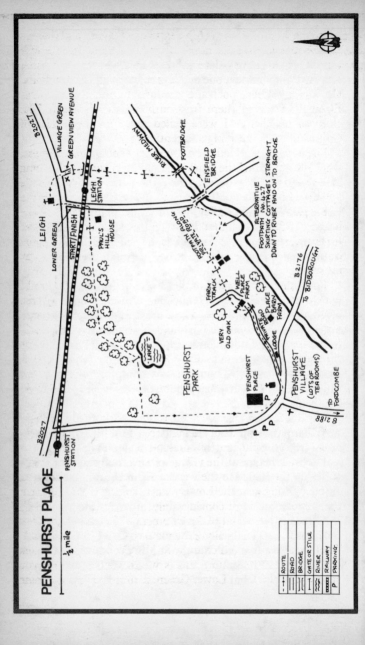

surviving from the fourteenth century in Britain, and there is a fine collection of arms in the crypt below. The main house was built as a Tudor palace and one of the earliest occupants was Sir Philip Sidney, one of the greatest of all Elizabethans. He was a soldier, poet and member of the Royal court. Elizabeth I stayed there frequently, as did James I. The children of Charles I were exiled there on the orders of Cromwell after the King's execution.

The house was added to on a number of occasions. Robert, who later became the Earl of Leicester, added the long gallery and nether gallery. In the eighteenth century the male line died out and the estate passed to the Shelleys, then the Lords de l'Isle and Dudley, who completed the work on the house. Today, Penshurst Place houses a fine collection of furniture and portraits as well as arms and armour. In the buttery at the rear of the main building there is a toy museum.

The Sidneys are buried in the chapel in the village church, which dates back to Saxon times although none of the original building remains. The church lies behind Leicester Square, named after the Earl, and is surrounded by beautifully preserved Tudor cottages and an ancient lych-gate. In the chapel are the remains of Sir William Sidney and there is a cross in memory of Thomas Boleyn, brother of Anne. Sir Philip Sidney is not buried here, however, but lies in St Paul's Cathedral.

The Place is surrounded by rolling park and woodland with many fine stands of ancient trees, and the whole area is cross-crossed by footpaths, making access easy.

The walk begins at the village of Leigh, pronounced 'lie'. It lies on the B2027 to the west of Hildenborough. There is ample parking near the Lower Green, on the B2027, or near the station, but park considerately.

There has been a lot of development in Leigh but many of the houses, especially along the main road, are centuries old. There is also a fine old church, St Mary's, which dates back to the thirteenth century and is worth visiting before you start your walk: from Lower Green, turn right along the main

The approach to St John's Church through the original Leicester Square in the centre of Penshurst village

road and walk along the pavement for a couple of hundred yards, past the village hall. The church has one marvellous window depicting the Virgin and Child dating from the fourteenth century, and a 300-year-old hour-glass mounted on the pulpit, said to have been used by clergy of old to time their sermons.

Returning to Lower Green and the station, walk under the railway bridge and up the hill until the road bears round to the left at Paul's Hill House. Beside the house you will see a footpath, signposted to Penshurst, which you follow.

I think this is the prettiest part of the walk. Although it is a gentle slope, it is not a difficult climb and it takes you through marvellous woodland and some spectacular oaks, many of them twisted after lightning strikes. If you are quiet as you make your way between the trees you might easily catch sight of the deer that roam the woodlands.

The path is clearly marked by the yellow footpath stickers on trees and stiles, and takes you between spectacular avenues of trees which centuries ago resounded to the noises of royal hunting parties.

The views from the top of the hill are breathtaking on a clear day as the path follows the park fencing. The path tends to follow straight lines and is well marked. You can soon see the great house beckoning you.

After you have visited the Place and the village, leave the church and turn left along the road for a short way, then turn into the private road running beside the gatehouse. Keep the walls of Penshurst Place on your left and follow the metalled road past the lane to Place Barn Farm, but stop here to look behind you at the magnificent view of Penshurst Place. Continue along the road until you see the sign for Well Place Farm. Here, cross the stile on the left-hand side of the road and follow the footpath (no.426) along the hedge, through a gate and then diagonally over the pasture to a gate on the far side of the field. You have to pass a massive old oak in the middle and cross a farm track before reaching the wooden gate. Go through the gate and walk along the footpath for about 75 yards before coming to a stile leading onto a private lane.

The lane leads you downhill to a cluster of cottages on your right. You can either keep on the lane until you hit the public road, then turn right for about 200 yards until you reach Ensfield Bridge, or you can skirt round the houses and follow the footpath (no.427) along the bank of the River Medway until you come to the bridge.

Cross the bridge and climb over the stile on the left-hand side of the road immediately the other side of the river. This is a continuation of footpath no.429 – the various footpaths are marked by numbered yellow signs that are quite easy to follow. Follow this path along the bank of the Medway for one field, go through a gate, turn sharp left over a stile, but stay on the 429 which takes you to a footbridge across the river. From the bridge you can see the tower of Leigh church, and the path is straight across two fields under the railway bridge. The path ends at a stile leading into Green View Avenue which takes you up to the village green.

Walk 10
CAMBER CASTLE
NEAR RYE, SUSSEX
5½ miles

Camber Castle was one of the sea defences built for Henry
VIII because of his fears of a French invasion. Similar
structures can be seen right along the south coast as far as
Falmouth. The central tower is thought to date from 1511,
but the five semi-circular bastions were built around 1540.

The castle is fascinating because it was one of the new era
of fortifications built from which to fire cannon and, in turn,
to withstand artillery attacks. The walls are deliberately low
to reduce the target area, and the gun-ports, once blocked
up, are now being opened again. The castle was abandoned in
1643, as the sea receded, and never saw military action. For
many years the castle has been closed to the public as efforts
are made to restore it. However, it is possible to walk round it
and building work has been arranged so that you can look
inside, even though at a distance and from behind barbed
wire.

This is a very flexible walk because nowhere is the going
tough; it is all on the flat, and it can be extended if you feel
like exploring a little more. As well as the castle, the walk can
be made to take in one of Britain's best bird reserves, a
restored windmill and a village swallowed up by the sea. It
also skirts one of the country's oldest towns. Binoculars are a
very good idea.

Start at the car park at the end of the Rye Harbour Road.
The car park stands below a Martello Tower that is now in a
dangerous condition so keep away. Martello Towers were

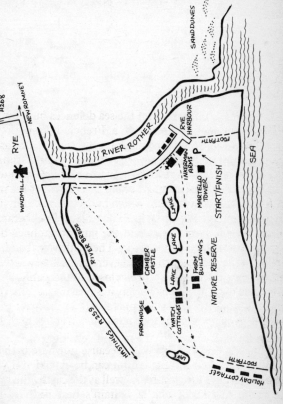

CAMBER CASTLE

|―――| 1 mile |

‑‑‑	ROUTE
	ROAD
	BRIDGE
P	PARKING
≈	RIVER

LONDON A268

RYE

NEW ROMNEY

WINDMILL

RIVER ROTHER

RYE HARBOUR

RIVER BREDE

INNKEEMAN ARMS

MARTELLO TOWER

START/FINISH

LAKE

LAKE

HASTINGS A259

FARMHOUSE

CAMBER CASTLE

LAKE

FARM BUILDINGS

NATURE RESERVE

WATCH COTTAGES

LAKE

FOOTPATH

HOLIDAY COTTAGES

SEA

SAND DUNES

built all along the south coast between 1805 and 1810 because of the threat of the invasion from France. The walls were more than five feet thick and each tower had a cannon mounted on the roof, which could be rotated to face the enemy over a wide front. But as things turned out, it never had to fire a shot.

From the car park, walk the few yards into Rye Harbour Road, and follow the pavement to just beyond the Inkerman Arms public house, where you reach the footpath sign pointing to the marshes. The church is on the other side of the footpath.

The first stage of the walk is not too glamorous as you travel through a small industrial complex making concrete and steel products for the engineering and building trades. This is soon left behind, however, and you are in glorious marshy countryside with huge lakes, formerly gravel pits, on your right, and the expanse of the marsh pastures spreading to the sea on your left. The footpath is easy to follow; keep the lakes to your right.

All this area lies withing the Rye Harbour Nature Reserve, run by the Sussex Naturalists Trust. Many important breeding sites can be found here, so keep to the footpath, especially during the spring and early summer. If you have young children with you, it is also important to keep them close to you: the lakes on your right are very deep, and the shingle banks leading to them are prone to subsidence.

On fine days, you should be able to see Camber Castle on your right and, beyond it, the magnificent sight of Rye which 500 years ago was one of the busiest sea-ports on the south coast. It is strange to think that much of the walk covers land that until a few hundred years ago was under the sea.

It is not possible to stray from the main path as long as you keep the castle and lakes to your right. When you come upon farm buildings, skirt round them, and then around two small cottages, Watch Cottages, which hug the shores of one of the lakes. A little while later, several footpaths meet.

If you wish, at this point you can make a detour down to Winchelsea Beach, just half a mile away – a good idea if you

Camber Castle, a reminder of more troubled times

want to have a paddle and picnic. Follow the path that runs alongside some holiday cottages and inspect these interesting buildings as you walk past. Several have been built using the shells of old railway carriages, and very fine they look, too. At the end of this path, climb steps over the sea-wall to get to the pebble beach.

Winchelsea Old Town was completely destroyed by a massive storm that rushed in from the sea in 1287. More than 300 buildings were said to have been destroyed and now lie buried beneath your feet. The new town of Winchelsea can be seen on the hill three miles to the west. It was built by Edward I, Lord Warder of the Cinque Ports, and work started in 1283 because the old port had already been hit by severe storms many times before. Both Rye and Winchelsea were members of the Cinque Ports, five trading sea-towns that dominated commerce in the Middle Ages; the other three were Sandwich, Rye and Romney, although Dover and Hastings were added to the list when some of the others went into decline.

After a paddle on the beach retrace your footsteps to the footpath crossroads, and continue on the path, now leading north, towards Camber Castle.

After inspecting the castle, follow the path that runs to the left of the perimeter fence, across the field to the houses by the Rye Harbour Road's junction with the A259, with the beautifully restored white windmill behind. The path is well trodden, although there are a number of gates to pass through. The footpath brings you out on the road by a bridge, turn right on this road and then you have about one and a half miles to walk down the road back to the car park. The road is straight; there is no pavement, but if you walk down the right-hand side you can have grass underfoot for most of the way.

If you wish to extend the walk still further, you can head south-east along the track which follows the right-hand bank of the River Rother. This track, a public footpath closed to motor vehicles, runs down to the shingle banks on the coast about three-quarters of a mile away. You can see a wide range of seabirds, waders, ducks and geese on this stretch, and watch the yachts and fishing boats. This extra walk is very well worthwhile if you are interested in birdwatching, and botany as well because there are many unusual plants to be spotted along the way. This detour could just as easily be done before the main walk.

Rye is a delightful town and well worth a visit, but I suggest you make this visit on the way home. There is ample car parking space in the town, and many cafés in the cobbled streets of ancient, oak-beamed buildings. After this walk, the idea of a cream tea will sound very appealing.

Walk 11
NUTLEY MILL
ASHDOWN FOREST, SUSSEX
5 miles

The windmill at Nutley is the oldest and smallest in Sussex. It was built in about 1675 at Crowborough, and was moved to its present site in 1810. It is very unusual being a post mill of the open trestle type and there are thought to be only five examples left in England. It has no fantail and was pushed to face into the wind with a tail pole.

The mill stopped working commercially in 1908 and fell into disrepair, but valiant work by the Uckfield and District Preservation Society in the late 1960s restored it to its former glory. The wheels began turning once more in 1971, driving two pairs of stones to grind corn again.

Although the windmill is open to the public only on the last Sunday of the month between Easter and the end of September, and on bank holidays, it is still a marvellous piece of history and worth viewing, even if from the outside.

Nutley itself is in the heart of Ashdown forest, one of the great unspoilt areas of the south-east where you can walk for mile after mile along footpaths and bridleways. Sadly, little remains of the once massive forest that stretched as far as the eye could see in every direction, but it still covers 6,500 acres of heath and woodland. Some of the land is still owned by the Army and is used as a training exercise area, but these areas are clearly marked and are still open to the public when not in use. The ancient forest that used to reach inland from the Kent coast to Hampshire, trapped between the North and South Downs, was rich in game and was a favourite

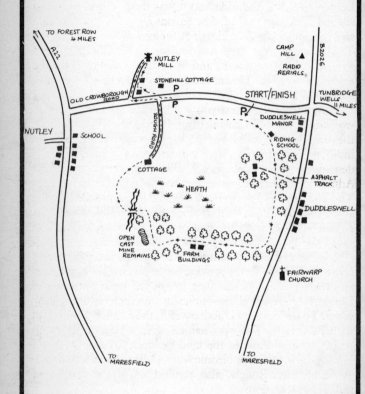

NUTLEY MILL

1 mile

TO FOREST ROW 4 MILES

A22

NUTLEY MILL

STONEHILL COTTAGE

P

OLD CROWBOROUGH ROAD

ROUGH ROAD

P

P

START/FINISH

CAMP HILL

RADIO AERIALS

B2026

TUNBRIDGE WELLS 11 MILES

DUDDLESWELL MANOR

RIDING SCHOOL

ASPHALT TRACK

DUDDLESWELL

NUTLEY

SCHOOL

COTTAGE

HEATH

OPEN CAST MINE REMAINS

FARM BUILDINGS

FAIRWARP CHURCH

TO MARESFIELD

TO MARESFIELD

--→ ROUTE
══ ROAD
⁓ GRASSLAND
∿ RIVER
P PARKING

playground for royal hunting parties. Unfortunately, the earth is also rich in iron, and trees were systematically felled over the centuries to fuel this industry. The habitat destruction also spelt the end of the wild hogs, wolves and huge herds of deer that roamed the forests. In Roman times the forest was known as Sylva Anderida and it was the Romans who first started to extract the ore. The Saxons named it Andreaswald and they began making clearings for agriculture. During the Tudor period, the area was known as the Weald, which simply means 'the wood', and this name is still used for the region between the Downs today, even though the trees have almost all gone.

Throughout the forest you will still see traces of the iron workings and open-cast smelting. During the Tudor period, the forest was exploited by both the shipbuilders and the iron industry. The Tudor kings, who created the English navy, demanded more timber to build more ships, while the Admiralty demanded more cannon to protect the vessels. The iron ore was dug from the clay and the trees felled for the smelting furnaces as well as shipbuilding. Fortunately, the advent of coal meant the end of timber-fired smelting and saved the few remaining pockets of woodland.

Another favourite pastime of the area was smuggling, and centuries ago the forest provided safe passage for smugglers and their pack horses as they journeyed from the coast to London. Duddleswell lies alongside one such old smuggling route. To the north of Duddleswell is the 650-feet Camp Hill with its aerials. This was named after a huge army camp which covered most of the land between Duddleswell and Nutley during the Napoleonic wars. Other place names, such as Campfields Rough, also remind us of the area's old military associations.

Throughout the area there are ponds and lakes, created by the damming of streams, used to provide water for the iron-making. The forest is very undulating and there can be some steep climbs, but they are avoided on this walk. The steep slopes result in water running quickly down to the valley floors, so these can be boggy after heavy rain and

Nutley Mill, one of the finest working windmills in Britain

sensible footwear is essential.

The forest is just over 35 miles from London and is best reached by taking the A22 south through East Grinstead, past Wych Cross, until just before you reach the village of Nutley. There you turn left for Duddleswell, which straddles the B2026 just to the east. There are parking spots by the roadside as well as in Duddleswell itself, but only stop if it is obvious you are allowed to do so. Illegal parking on the narrow roads can cause enormous traffic problems.

The best parking is off the Old Crowborough Road, a right-hand turning on the northern outskirts of Nutley. Follow the Old Crowborough Road for about half a mile and you will see car parks on both sides of the road. Park south of the road and to start the walk follow the bridlepath running parallel to it. After about half a mile, this path swings to the right, past a large riding school on the left, and then for some distance it again runs parallel to a road, this time the B2026. Cross over the asphalt track leading to houses, staying on the bridleway. You will see the steeple of Fairwarp Church ahead of you and to the left and as soon as this is hidden by the trees, on a down slope, the bridleway splits. Take the smaller, right-hand fork.

The path goes through trees and then splits again. The bridleway on the right zig-zags over the heath towards Nutley Mill, but for our main, longer, walk stick to the left-hand fork. This takes you past some farm buildings on the left and up a gentle slope to the top of a small hill. In the spring time this area is ablaze with the colour of bluebells and broom, and is a haven for wildlife.

As the path descends a slightly steeper slope it splits and you take the right-hand turning, which veers round to the right. Almost immediately on the left you pass an open-cast iron working. Stick to this path with the houses of Nutley over the valley on the left.

The path then meets another at a T-junction. Turn left, and follow the slope down and cross a footbridge over a stream. Stick to this path, with a chain-link fence on the left. It climbs up the hill with pasture land on the right. This area is popular with horse riders – keep an eye out for them – so it can be quite muddy. Stay on the path until you pass a cottage on the right and then join the bridleway which runs parallel to a rough road linking the cottage to the Old Crowborough Road. The bridleway takes you almost to the road, and you will emerge opposite the entrance to Stonehill Cottage.

Turn left on the road and walk along the verge for about 300 yards to the entrance to Nutley Mill on the right-hand side of the road. The mill is about 300 yards up the lane, which cars are not allowed to use. Having visited the mill go back to the road, turn left and go past the bridleway up which you walked. Just beyond it, there is a car park on the right. A path leaves the bottom of this car park, and you follow it until it meets a broad bridleway, where you turn left. Follow this bridlepath, which runs parallel to the road and takes you back to your car.

Walk 12
CISSBURY RING
WEST SUSSEX
5 miles

Cissbury is one of the most extensive hill forts in Britain and dates from the late Iron Age, about 200 years before Christ. It was occupied before the fortifications were built, certainly since the fifth century BC, by hunters who mined here for their flints. The evidence of their open-cast mining is everywhere. Inside the fort's spectacular earthworks has been found a Bronze Age burial chamber, and there is evidence that the Romans used the fortifications as a protection against the Saxon pirates who attacked the channel towns in the third century. A Romano-British circular shrine was also discovered here.

It is quite easy to see why the local people chose Cissbury for their fort. The steep sides leading to the summit would have tired any attackers, and they would have been easily picked off by stones or arrows as they negotiated earthworks and deep ditches. The ditch runs for more than 2,000 yards around the site and there is a series of earth banks, the tallest being 20 feet high.

The origin of the name Cissbury is uncertain but it could have come from a Saxon chief called Aelle who settled in the area in 477. He had three sons, one of whom was called Cissa.

From the summit there are magnificent views on a clear day and it is quite possible to see along the coast from Beachy Head in the east to the Isle of Wight in the west. If you turn inland and look to the north, you will see Chanctonbury Ring, a circle of beech trees planted in the eighteenth century

63

CISSBURY RING

1 mile

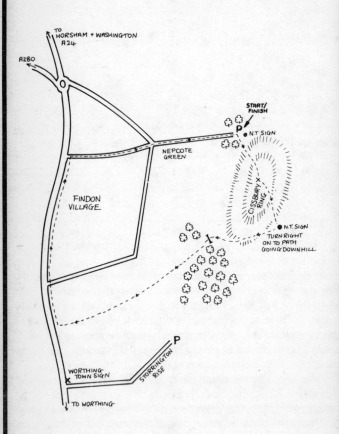

TO HORSHAM + WASHINGTON A24

A280

O

START/ FINISH

P

N.T. SIGN

NEPCOTE GREEN

FINDON VILLAGE

CISSBURY RING

N.T. SIGN
TURN RIGHT
ON TO PATH
GOING DOWNHILL

P

WORTHING TOWN SIGN

STORRINGTON RISE

TO WORTHING

Key	
---•---	ROUTE
═══	ROAD
P	PARKING
/////	HILL STEEP

N

The path to the top of Cissbury Ring, whose summit provides one of the finest viewpoints in the south-east

on the summit of a neighbouring hill. You can also see the spire of Chichester Cathedral from this vantage point, which can be windy and sometimes muddy, so a jumper is advisable even in the summer, and boots are a good idea all year round.

The site is owned by the National Trust and a lot of work is going on to prevent erosion of the paths. Steps have been built and you should stick to the many clearly marked paths rather than make your own way across the Ring.

Although the basic walk is about 2½ miles long, it is very adaptable and can be extended to take in the delightful quaint village of Findon. Or you can simply walk all the way round the Ring, taking in its breathtaking views on a fine day. Even when the weather is not good, it is a remarkable place to visit.

Approach by the A24, through the village of Findon. You will see a lane signposted to Cissbury Ring and you should follow this for about one and a half miles until you reach a small free parking area immediately below the summit of the Ring.

It is simply a matter of walking up the hill past the National Trust signs onto the Ring itself. The whole area is crisscrossed by footpaths and bridleways and one of the best ways of exploring is simply to follow the perimeter fence right round. But if you want to do the whole walk rather than just circumnavigate the fort, descend the Ring on the side opposite the car park, go past the National Trust sign and take the path leading to the right. This takes you along the edge of the fort. Keep walking downhill, skirting the wood on your left, until you reach the main A24. Turn right and follow the path running along the road before turning right again. This will take you into Findon, which is a charming village and well worth exploring. You cannot get lost because you will see the sign pointing the way to 'Cissbury Ring car park number one.' Follow this as far as Nepcote Green and then use the bridleway on the right-hand side of the lane to take you back to your car.

Walk 13
THE GRANGE
NEAR NORTHINGTON, HANTS
6½ miles

The Grange is said to be the finest building in Hampshire and the one with the most commanding position. It was one of the first to be inspired by the neo-classical style of architecture, and is one of the finest examples of it in Europe. Built in the early nineteenth century on the site of the previous house, it represents architect William Wilkins' masterpiece, which sadly was then allowed to fall slowly into disrepair. Fortunately, the government stepped in early in the 1970s, when only the empty shell remained, and saved it.

The house is still empty but the facade has been well restored, and while the public cannot enter the building, they can visit the grounds (except on Sunday mornings) to view its magnificent exterior and the surrounding parkland. There is still an Ionic portico nearby at the entrance to the Orangery, an early glass and cast-iron building.

The walk starts at Abbotstone Down from the car park on the B3046. Abbotstone Down lies to the north of the village of Alresford on the A31. It is now a large area of downland, ideal for picnics, which covers 32 acres and is one of the few remaining fragments of downland plateau in Hampshire. It includes the remains of an iron-age hill fort known as Oliver's Battery. In the surrounding woods it is possible to see fallow and roe deer, and the downland flora includes more than fifty varieties of mosses and liverworts.

The circular ditch and bank of the ancient fort are still visible, although it is thought that the earthworks were used

THE GRANGE

1 mile

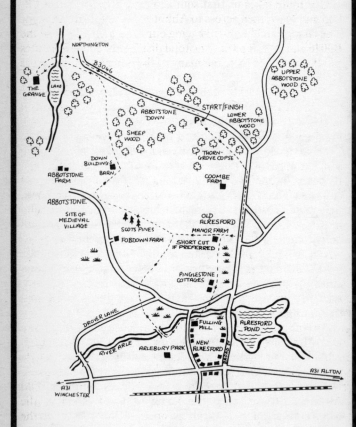

NORTHINGTON

THE GRANGE

LAKE

B3046

UPPER ABBOTSTONE WOOD

START/FINISH

P

LOWER ABBOTSTONE WOOD

ABBOTSTONE DOWN

SHEEP WOOD

THORN-GROVE COPSE

DOWN BUILDINGS

BARN

ABBOTSTONE FARM

COOMBE FARM

ABBOTSTONE

SITE OF MEDIEVAL VILLAGE

OLD ALRESFORD

MANOR FARM

SCOTS PINES

FOBDOWN FARM

SHORT CUT IF PREFERRED

PINGLESTONE COTTAGES

DROVER LANE

FULLING MILL

ALRESFORD POND

RIVER ARLE

ARLEBURY PARK

NEW ALRESFORD

ROAD H.

A31 ALTON

A31 WINCHESTER

--→	ROUTE
	ROAD
	BRIDGE
≈≈	RIVER
	GRASSLAND
P	PARKING
▪▪▪▪	RAILWAY

for agricultural rather than military purposes. Locals believe the fort gets its name from Oliver Cromwell, who fought a major battle at nearby Cheriton, but it is not known whether he visited Abbotstone Down or not.

Our route takes us first south to the village of Alresford, Old and New, then across to Abbotstone, before heading for The Grange and finally retracing our steps a little back to the B3046 and the car park. The total distance of about 6½ miles can be shortened by using many of the other paths that cross the area covered.

The walk is another of those created by Hampshire County Council's Recreation Department and is clearly waymarked in yellow for most of the route, then switching to blue signs for the leg to The Grange and back to the car park.

From the car park follow the yellow waymark signs leading south towards the village of Alresford. The path takes you through Thorngrove Copse, taking its name from the word coppice. These small clumps of trees were very common throughout England until earlier this century, and consisted mostly of hazel trees. Every eight or ten years the trees would be cut back to the ground to promote the growth of poles which could then be harvested for thatching poles, stakes for fences and so on. Many coppices have unfortunately disappeared because they are no longer economic to harvest, and they are often grubbed out to make fields larger and therefore more easily managed.

After the copse, the path joins the B3046, which leads into Old Alresford. This is a delightful village with a church rebuilt in the eighteenth and nineteenth centuries, and a village green with a stream running across it. The Mother's Union was founded here in 1876 by Mary Summer. Old Alresford House, once the home of Lord Rodney, the eighteenth-century admiral, is open to the public in the summer.

Alresford is split into two, Old and New, separated by about a mile of land which used to be a reservoir created by Bishop Godfrey de Lucy. Known as Alresford Pond, it was built in the twelfth century to make the River Itchen more

One of the many architectural delights to be found around Abbotstone

navigable from Southampton to nearby Bishop Sutton. There is still a causeway crossing the area and while the pond used to be famous for eels three hundred years ago, the waterlogged fields are now noted for their watercress beds.

New Alresford, which sprawls down to the A31 in the south, has a very long history despite its name. Before the Norman Conquest it belonged to the Bishops of Winchester but little remains of the old town. A number of devastating fires in the seventeenth and eighteenth centuries destroyed most of the original wood buildings. The most picturesque part of the village is around Broad Street, which contains some fine old buildings. You can see the plaque to Mary Russell Mitford, who wrote *Our Village*, who was born here. At the bottom of Broad Street there is a medieval bridge.

The church is also worth a visit. It was built in the nineteenth century in Perpendicular style and contains two Anglo-Saxon roods. In the graveyard you can see the tombstones of Napoleonic prisoners of war who died in the village.

From New Alresford follow the yellow signs back to the River Arle and fulling mill. In medieval times Alresford boasted one of the largest sheep fairs in the country, and the fleeces were washed and treated at the mill before being home-spun.

Our path then follows the River Arle for a short distance before crossing it and joining the lane leading to Abbotstone. The whole of this area is criss-crossed by a number of ancient byways, many of them old drove roads. The one that enters Abbotstone Down from the north is an ancient sheepwalk dating back to at least Saxon times, while the bridleway where our walk started follows the old road to Winchester.

Sheep raised on the downland were taken to market along these paths and provided the wealth of the neighbourhood. Today, modern intensive arable farming has taken over from livestock, and cereals now grow where sheep once grazed.

Although there is little to be seen of Abbotstone today, the depression and embankments on either side of the road give some impression of what the layout of the medieval village must have looked like. The village once covered more than 15 acres and was the centre of a thriving farming community with its own church. It went into decline in the fifteenth century due to both the collapse of the wool trade in the area and the Black Death.

From Abbotstone follow the yellow arrows as if heading back to the car park and then turn left on to the blue waymarked path which takes you up to the B3046 and then on to The Grange.

From The Grange you retrace your tracks to the B3046 and follow this until you return to the car park.

Walk 14
ST NICHOLAS' CHURCH
BOARHUNT, NEAR SOUTHWICK, HANTS
4½ miles

This Saxon church dates from about 1064 and is one of the finest examples of its type in the country, remaining virtually unspoilt. It still retains its original dimensions and the walls are two and a half feet thick. Sadly, some restoration was carried out in the nineteenth century, and only one of the original windows remains. The interior furnishing and bell-cote date from the nineteenth century. One of the church's star attractions is the massive hollow yew tree in the churchyard, believed to be at least 1,000 years old and with a girth of more than 30 feet. With the old manor house, now Manor Farm, and Boarhunt Mill, the church is all that remains of a once thriving village which became deserted during the Middle Ages. Three mills were mentioned in the Domesday Book as being in the vicinity. The existing mill, on the site of one of these, ceased operating in 1928 and the mill race is now a private garden. The Wallington river which passes the mill has several tributaries and where the upper and lower Wallington join, near Newman's bridge, was the site of Little Applestede, part of the medieval manor of Applestede, forerunner of Southwick village.

The walk starts from the village of Southwick, which lies about three miles north of Portsmouth. There is a large lay-by car park to the east of the village on the A333. The village has seen some development in recent years but there are still fine old buildings, many of them dating back to the eighteenth century, some of them thatched. St James's

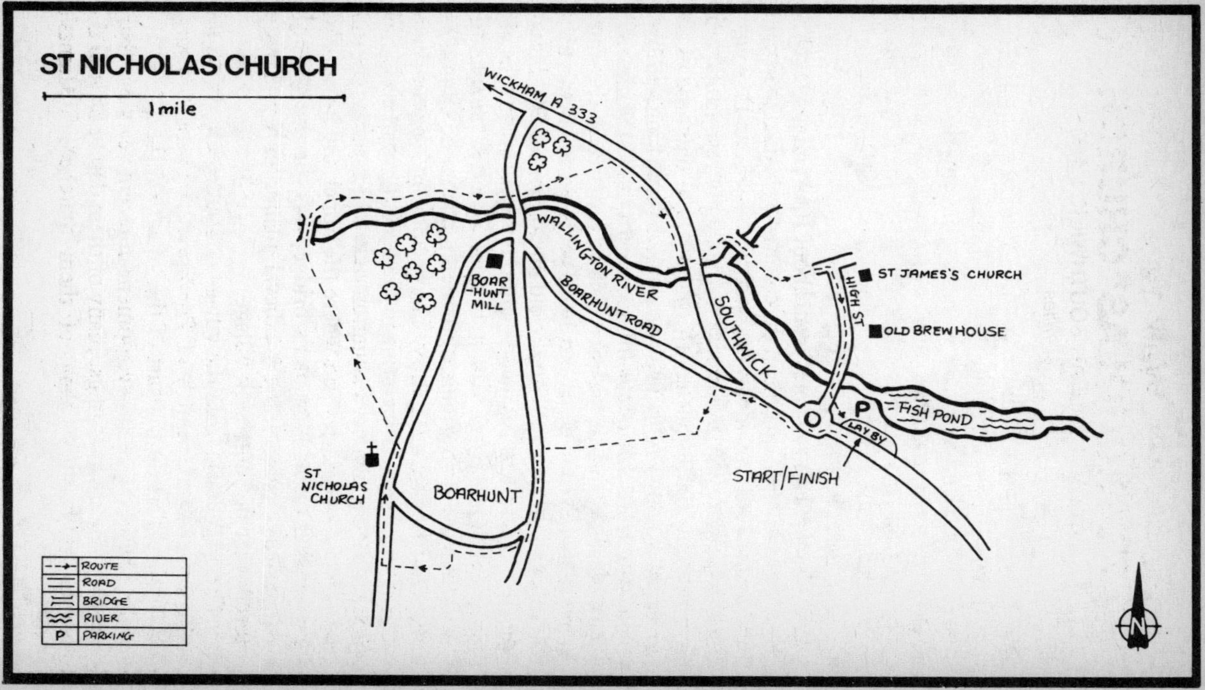

ST NICHOLAS CHURCH

1 mile

N

ST JAMES'S CHURCH

OLD BREW HOUSE

HIGH ST

FISH POND

P

LAZY

START/FINISH

SOUTHWICK

WALLINGTON RIVER

BOARHUNT ROAD

WICKHAM B 333

BOAR-HUNT MILL

BOARHUNT

ST NICHOLAS CHURCH

→→	ROUTE
‖‖	ROAD
≈	BRIDGE
≋	RIVER
P	PARKING

Church in Southwick is perpendicular in style but there are still sections to be seen dating from other periods. There is a fine eighteenth-century painted altar piece and a seventeenth-century gallery and pulpit. The church officially dates from 1566 and its full name is St James-without-the-priory Gate. It was officially a 'peculiar', that is a church that was outside the local bishop's jurisdiction.

John Whyte is buried here with his wife, and the brasses which cover the top of their tomb attract collectors of brass rubbings from many countries. It was John Whyte who acquired the Augustinian Priory duing the Dissolution of the Monasteries. The Priory had been founded in Portchester in 1133 but moved to Southwick in 1146. Almost all the buildings were destroyed by Whyte, who used the materials to build his manor house around the prior's lodgings. That house was destroyed by fire and the one that replaced it was also burnt to the ground. The present Southwick House dates from the nineteenth century and was used as Eisenhower's headquarters for the planning of the D-Day invasions during the last war.

Southwick is one of Hampshire's many privately owned villages and it remains largely unspoilt, thanks to many centuries of careful estate management. The village green has been restored, brick pavements laid down and telephone poles and wires have been removed from view in an attempt to recapture a feel of yesteryear. The old brewhouse of the Golden Lion is also being restored as a brewery museum, and its original vats and machinery are being displayed.

I have chosen this walk because it is one of the best sign-posted routes I have ever followed. The walk, like others around Southwick, was prepared by the Recreation Department of Hampshire County Council in co-operation with the Southwick Estate. My thanks to them for allowing me to use it. Strong boots or wellingtons are recommended.

The route starts at the roundabout where the High Street and A333 meet and you follow the Boarhunt Road until you meet the footpath marked with the red arrows; simply follow these indicators throughout. This footpath used to be a

Boarhunt Mill, one of the few remaining signs of a once thriving medieval village

causeway, elevated above the fields as a means of access from Southwick to St Nicholas Church at Boarhunt.

The walk is both easy and pleasant, passing through quiet, undisturbed English countryside, yet you will be enjoying this tranquillity only a few miles from the bustle of Portsmouth. Keep an eye open for traces on the ground of buildings long since disappeared, faint echoes from the Middle Ages.

There are other walks of various lengths around Southwick, including one to the north, skirting Walton Heath, and a longer one to the north and east, through part of the ancient Forest of Bere. Like our chosen walk, these are excellently waymarked.

Walk 15
THE WHITE HORSE OF THE RIDGEWAY
UFFINGTON, BERKS
6½ miles

This is a walk that can be varied according to how far you want to go. It is also a very good introduction to the Ridgeway long distance path which runs for 85 miles from Overton Mill near the stone circle of Avebury, though the North Wessex Downs, across the Thames at Goring and through the Chilterns to Ivinghoe Beacon. The path is of enormous historical interest because it follows as closely as possible the route of the ancient Wessex Ridgeway and the Icknield Way. Throughout its length there are archaeological sites to be investigated and very special flora and fauna as the path wends its way through the chalk uplands.

White Horse Mill, at 856 feet the highest point on the Berkshire Downs, can also be reached by the Portway, an old Roman road. To the north of White Horse Hill is Dragon Hill, where legend has it that St George slew the dragon. The whole area is steeped in legend and mystery, and was the romping ground for the characters of Thomas Hughes in the early chapters of *Tom Brown's Schooldays*. The strangely shaped White Horse, known as the Uffington White Horse because of the village which lies in the vale to the north, is 360 feet long and about 130 feet high. Locals insist it was carved by King Alfred, but most archaeologists think it dates back to at least the Iron Age. No-one knows for sure, which adds to the mystery of the area.

The route is easy to follow and well walked, especially the Ridgeway which can be very popular at weekends. The

THE WHITE HORSE OF THE RIDGEWAY

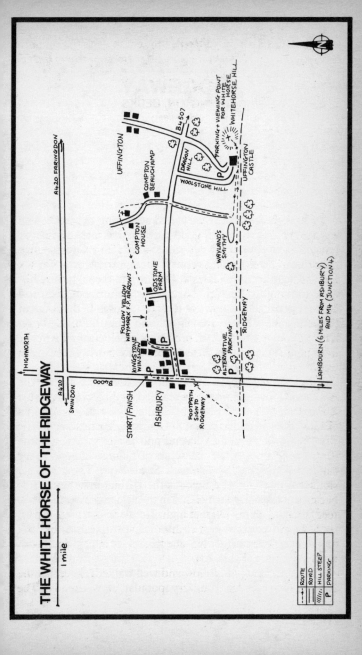

1 mile

N

+·+·+·+	ROUTE
———	ROAD
/////	HILL STEEP
P	PARKING

A420 FARINGDON

A4200 Highworth

SWINDON A420

Ashbury

B4000

START/FINISH

KINGSTONE WINSLOW

FOLLOW YELLOW WAYMARK F.P. ARROWS

COMPTON HOUSE

ODSTONE FARM

COMPTON BEAUCHAMP

UFFINGTON

B4507

DRAGON HILL

WOOLSTONE HILL

PARKING + VIEWING POINT FOR WHITE HORSE

WHITEHORSE HILL

UFFINGTON CASTLE

WAYLAND'S SMITHY

RIDGEWAY

FOOTPATH SIGN TO RIDGEWAY

ALTERNATIVE PARKING

LAMBOURN (6 MILES FROM ASHBURY) AND M4 (JUNCTION 4)

walking is not strenuous and even the climb up to the summit of White Horse Hill is not too taxing. Because much of the walk is on chalk, though, this can cause problems. Chalk becomes more cloggy after rain and can be quite slippery, so care is needed, but nowhere is a fall likely to be dangerous.

The easiest way to get to Ashbury, where the walk begins, is to follow the B4000 either south from its turn-off with the A420 Swindon to Fraingdon road, or northwards after turning off the M4 at junction 14. From the monastery head for Lambourn and then take the clearly signposted Ashbury Road. You can then park – considerately – in the village or in the car park of the pub, which makes an excellent refreshment stop. It is worth spending some time in Ashbury. The old manor house, now a farm, dates from the fifteenth century. The church has a Norman south door, and the nave arcades are from the Perpendicular period.

Walk south on the B4000 until a sign to the Ridgeway directs you off to the right. After about half a mile of clearly marked path, you turn left onto the Ridgeway path itself and this leads you straight past Wayland's Smithy to Uffington Castle, a hill fort. A little further on is White Horse Hill. Uffington fort dates back to at least 500BC and some historians believe that the Ridgeway path which passes it is the oldest road in Europe and could date back to the last Ice Age.

After exploring the hilltop, the horse and fort, make your way back down the Ridgeway until you come to Wayland's Smithy again. This is a megalithic long barrow, or burial chamber. Legend has it that the smith manufactured swords which made the owners invincible. He was reputed to be smith to the Saxon gods, and after his death it was said he would still re-shoe the horses of travellers left there overnight, provided a coin was left by the burial mound.

From the Smithy there is a clearly marked metalled path running northwards. Follow this and cross over the B4507 into Compton Beauchamp, past Compton House and on up to the church. Take the footpath which starts just to the right of the church gate. After going through a farm gate straight ahead, bear to the right slightly and cross two fields, heading

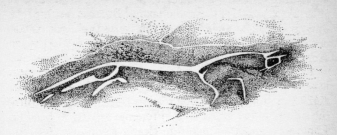

The White Horse of Uffington, a relic from ancient times but still a landmark for miles

for a gate in the corner of the second. Follow the yellow arrow waymarks.

Keep to the left-hand side of this field, crossing the stiles at the far side, and then walk past Odstone Farm which should be on your left. Keep going straight on through the gates and follow the path round to the left as it keeps to the line of the electricity poles. This path broadens out and eventually emerges into a lane at Kingstone Winslow. Turn left and then right into a lane which takes you back to Ashbury and the car.

If you follow the route as suggested, the whole walk will take you two to three hours, depending on how much time you spend exploring. If you do not want to walk so far, you can simply do the circular walk from Ashbury to Wayland's Smithy burial chamber and then on up to Compton Beauchamp and back to Ashbury. This will save you two miles of walking, but you should then drive along the B4507 for just over two miles until you see the small side road on your right which will take you up to the White Horse. After all, you cannot travel into the area without spending some time examining this mysterious huge carving.

Walk 16
BOTANICAL GARDENS
OXFORD
2 miles

These are the oldest botanical gardens in Britain, having been founded in 1621 by Henry Danvers, Earl of Danby. Every day there is something new to see: they even cultivate weeds for botanical study. There is a fine main gateway, designed by Nicholas Stone in the manner of Inigo Jones, the lawns border the softly flowing River Cherwell, and goldfish swim beneath the dripping fountain of the lily pond. The towers of Magdalen and Merton Colleges provide a superb backdrop. As Jan Morris wrote, 'There can be few better places in England for the contemplation of flowers.'

Although Oxford itself is now quite a sprawling town, the centre has remained unchanged and the colleges still dominate the life of the community. Oxford University is the second oldest in Europe, after the Sorbonne in Paris, and the first records of academic life date back to the twelfth century. The first chancellor was appointed in 1214 but its great boost came during the latter part of the thirteenth century when all foreign students were ordered to leave the Sorbonne, many of whom made their way to Oxford. Although many of the colleges were founded by religious institutions, others were established thanks to the generosity of wealthy, influential patrons.

Despite its size, Oxford has more than enough green areas to enjoy and you can picnic down by the Thames if the weather is pleasant, stroll through the municipal gardens and the grounds of some of the colleges, or just wander the streets

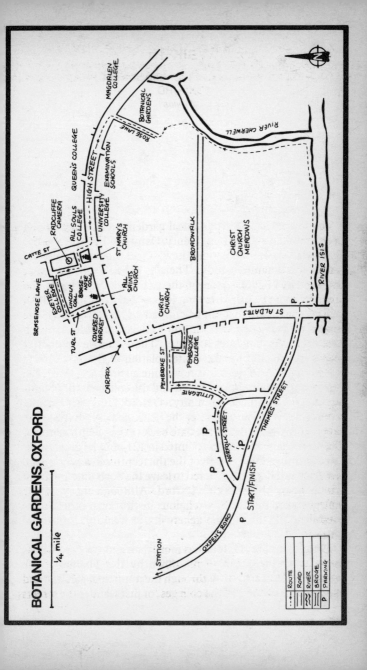

BOTANICAL GARDENS, OXFORD

¼ mile

••••	ROUTE
▦	ROAD
▒	RIVER
⫴	BRIDGE
P	PARKING

STATION

OXPENS ROAD

START/FINISH

NORFOLK STREET

THAMES STREET

LITTLEGATE

PEMBROKE ST

PEMBROKE COLLEGE

CARFAX

TURL ST

COVERED MARKET

BRASENOSE LANE

EXETER COLLEGE

LINCOLN COLL

BRASE-NOSE COLL

ALL SAINTS CHURCH

CHRIST CHURCH

ST ALDATES

RADCLIFFE CAMERA

CATTE ST

ALL SOULS COLLEGE

ST MARY'S CHURCH

UNIVERSITY COLLEGE

HIGH STREET

QUEEN'S COLLEGE

EXAMINATION SCHOOLS

MAGDALEN COLLEGE

BOTANICAL GARDENS

ROSE LANE

RIVER CHERWELL

BROADWALK

CHRIST CHURCH MEADOWS

RIVER ISIS

admiring the magnificent buildings. All the colleges are open to the public but some only in the afternoons.

The walk is a rather twisting circular route and although it covers only a couple of miles, it could take you many hours if you want to do it justice and see all the colleges on the route. I have not included some of the colleges because they are off the walk, but town walks have the virtue that provided you can follow a street map, you can always shorten or lengthen the journey depending on how you feel. It is quite easy to cut a corner off the walk by taking another street, or to extend it by taking in one of the outlying colleges. This is one of those town walks which prove that it is possible to go walking as a family in an urban environment and get as much pleasure from looking at buildings as you can from being in open countryside.

Start your walk in one of the many car parks in the Oxpens area, to the south-west of the city centre. Walk east along Oxpens Road and Thames Street to St Aldates. Cross St Aldates and in the wall at the far side of a small car park in front of you is a gate into Christ Church Meadow. Go through the gate and turn right, following the path down to the River Thames – or the Isis as it is named where it flows through Oxford.

Follow the river with the beautiful Christ Church Meadow on your left. The Meadow now seems to be safe from senseless plans to build a main road across it. Keep left on the path as it swings round where the Cherwell joins the Isis and follow the bank of the Cherwell until a wide path called the Broadwalk joins from the left. Just after this junction, your path bears left to the end of Rose Lane. Walk down this lane to the High Street, turn right and the Botanical Gardens are on your right.

Ahead of you when you when you leave the Gardens is Magdalen College, founded by William of Waynflete in 1458. It is one of the largest colleges and one of its most prominent features is the Perpendicular bell tower, completed in 1509 after seventeen years. The main quadrangle is still surrounded by cloisters. The New Buildings, just to the

Oxford, the city of learning, history and architecture, represented by Christ Church's Tom Tower

north and dating from the eighteenth century, overlook Magdalen Grove, a deer park, where open-air plays and recitals are still performed during the summer.

Turn left up the High Street, passing first the Examination Schools on your left, then Queen's College on your right, University College on your left and All Souls College on the right. All University exams take place in the Examination Schools, whose detailed, even fussy architecture is typical of the late Victorian period. Queen's College is named after Philippa of Hainault, Edward III's queen, and has a long tradition of attracting students from the North of England. University College was the first college to be endowed, in 1249. All Souls was founded in 1437–8 to commemorate Henry V and the soldiers who fell at the battle of Agincourt, and its ornately carved gateway onto the High Street is one of the splendours of Oxford.

Turn right into Catte Street, between All Souls and the

University Church of St Mary's, and follow it into Radcliffe Square. Walk round the splendidly domed Radcliffe Camera to the diagonally opposite corner and take Brasenose Lane between Brasenose College on the left and Exeter College on the right. Brasenose got its name from the brass door-knocker which used to grace its oak door. Exeter chapel was built by Sir Gilbert Scott and contains many fine tapestries.

At the end of Brasenose Lane turn left into Turl Street, past Lincoln College, whose library now occupies the fine church of All Saints at the end of Turl Street. Turn right there back into the High Street and the covered market, with its many interesting shops, is now on your right.

At the next crossroads, which is called Carfax (from the Latin 'quadrifurcus', meaning 'four ways') and is the centre of Oxford, turn left into St Aldates. 200 yards down on the left is Christ Church, the largest and best-known of all the colleges. It was founded by Cardinal Wolsey and was originally known as Cardinal College when it was licensed by Henry VIII in 1525. It has one of the finest positions in Oxford with marvellous views over Christ Church Meadow to the Isis and the Cherwell. The Front Quadrangle is known as Tom Quad, because of the great bell hanging in the tower over the gateway dedicated to St Thomas of Canterbury. It is the largest bell in Oxford weighing six tons. The college is also famed for its magnificent timbered-roof hall and its priceless collection of portraits. The Cardinal created a new see in 1542 so that the college could have its own cathedral, and the Church of St Frideswide is the smallest cathedral in Britain, though still beautiful.

Cross St Aldates opposite Christ Church into Pembroke Square, where Pembroke College is situated. It is built in a restrained Jacobean style with some Victorian re-modelling. From the north-west corner of Pembroke Square, Pembroke Street leads you to Littlegate, where you turn left and so back to the complex of car parks at Oxpens.

Walk 17
WHITE SHEET HILL
MERE, WILTSHIRE
5 miles

White Sheet Hill gets its name from the colour of its chalk and from the old English word 'sceot', meaning 'steep-sided'. At the top of the hill is an Iron Age fort which originally covered at least 15 acres. To the south and west, because of the steep hill slopes, there is only a single defensive ditch, but to the north and east, where the land is much less steep, there is a series of three ditches which must have proved a formidable barrier.

A neolithic camp has also been discovered just to the north of the fort. It was excavated 35 years ago and covers four acres. It dates back at least 2,500 years and is believed to have been a meeting place rather than a defensive position. Some of the articles discovered during the excavation can be seen in Mere Museum.

From the summit of White Sheet Hill there are marvellous views in all directions and you can see your route home, whichever path you take. There are also fine views of Stourhead, to the west of Mere.

Mere itself is not a large town but it has plenty of history and there are many walks in the area, taking in many places of archaeological and historical interest. The town lies near the borders with Dorset and Somerset. Many of the cottages are built of local stone, much of it quarried on the outskirts of town, but a number of buildings utilised stone from the new vanished castle which once dominated the town from its site on the top of Castle Hill. Nothing remains of the

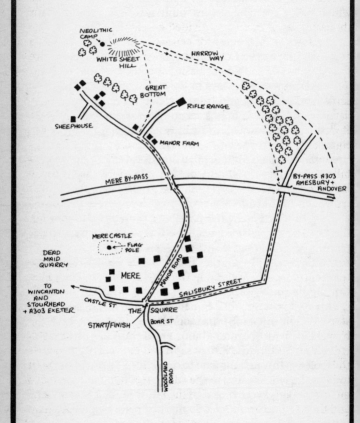

WHITE SHEET HILL

|—————————|
1 mile

NEOLITHIC CAMP

WHITE SHEET HILL

HARROW WAY

GREAT BOTTOM

RIFLE RANGE

SHEEPHOUSE

MANOR FARM

MERE BY-PASS

BY-PASS A303 AMESBURY + ANDOVER

MERE CASTLE
FLAG POLE

DEAD MAID QUARRY

MERE

MANOR ROAD

SALISBURY STREET

TO WINCANTON AND STOURHEAD + A303 EXETER

CASTLE ST

THE SQUARE

START/FINISH

BOAR ST

WOODLAND ROAD

- - -+- - -	ROUTE
≡≡≡	ROAD
⌣⌣	BRIDGE
/////	HILL STEEP
⊢——⊣	GATE OR STILE

fortifications today but the site is still worth visiting both for the spectacular views it affords of the town and the surrounding countryside, and to get an impression of the defensive position it occupied. The flagpole on the summit stands as a marker for miles around.

The town is surrounded by a number of other steep hills which, with forts or castles built on their summits, for thousands of years have provided a defensive ring.

The town of Mere has for centuries been important as a coaching stop on the London to Exeter road, but long before that there was a settlement beside the Harrow Way. This is one of the oldest trackways in Britain, which stretches right across southern England from Kent to Devon and certainly dates back at least 2,500 years to the early Stone Age. The Romans used it to move their troops quickly and in the eighteenth century it was used as a coaching route.

The area around Mere is open downland and steep wooded hills. There are many interesting places to visit nearby including Stourhead – a National Trust property about three miles west of the town – and Woodlands Manor to the south.

To get to Mere, take the A303 which used to run through the town but now by-passes it to the north. There is ample parking in the town in free car parks, and the one off Salisbury Street has toilets. There is also a tourist information centre by The Square, in the middle of the town, which can supply details of the town and other walks in the area.

Our walk starts in The Square. After an inspection of the stone buildings, walk up Manor Road. Follow it over the by-pass until just beyond Manor Farm. Beside a cottage you will see an MOD Rifle Range sign; and the walk now follows the footpath through the gate to the right. For a time the path follows the lane leading to the rifle range but keep the fence on your left and veer round to the left through a second gate and then on and up the clearly marked path which takes you to the summit of White Sheet Hill.

As you walk up to the summit you pass through Great Bottom; this whole area is now a nature reserve because of its rich flora, which accommodates many species of butterfly.

The magnificent grounds of Stourhead, a National Trust property which lies to the west of Mere and White Sheet Hill

From the summit of White Sheet Hill go to the right along the clearly defined path along the summit of the ridge. Continue along this for about two miles, always with Mere in the valley on your right. The path follows the route of the Harrow Way until a clearly marked footpath branches away downhill on your right. Follow this path down, skirting the fields, until you come to a stile. Cross the stile and follow the path down to the road. Turn right, go under the by-pass, and follow this road back into Mere and your car.

Mere Castle, built in 1253 by Richard, Earl of Cornwall, was constructed of stone and wood. It is said that 200 giant oaks from the Forest of Blackmore were felled for the project, while the stone came from nearby quarries. The castle was almost 400 feet long and over 100 feet wide and had six towers. But within 400 years it had become a ruin and the stones were being used for local housing.

Much of this stone can still be seen today in the lovely old cottages and houses. The Old Ship Inn in Castle Street is also worth a visit because of its eighteenth century wrought-iron sign made by Kingston Avery, who also made the clock in the Church of St Michael's.

The Ship Inn, like the Talbot by The Square, was a thriving coaching inn. In 1850 the coach trip from Mere to London took 24 hours and passengers paid 30 shillings to travel inside or 16 shillings to ride on top. The Ship Inn was formerly the house of Sir John Coventry, a Royalist and member of the Long Parliament, while Charles II, heavily disguised as a servant during his flight from the Battle of Worcester in 1651, stayed at the Talbot.

Apart from its clock, the Church of St Michael's is worth visiting. Much of it dates back to 1450, although there are still traces dating back to the eleventh century. The Jacobean pews date from the early seventeenth century and there are two fine brasses in the south chapel; one is of Sir John Bettesthorne and dates from 1398. There is an alabaster tablet dating from 1325, on the north wall of the sanctuary, which was discovered in the garden of a nearby house in 1878. The tablet depicts the Adoration of the Magi and may have originally hung in the chapel of Mere Castle.

Also worth visiting is the fifteenth century Chantry House in Church Street, once a school run by the Dorset poet, William Barnes.

If you have the time, a visit to the National Trust property at Stourhead, three miles to the west, is rewarding. Lying in the village of Stourton, the landscaped gardens of Stourhead were laid out between 1741 and 1750 and include lakes, temples, grottoes, and ornate bridges, and many rare plants and trees. The house, which like the garden is open to the public for a small charge, was begun in 1721 by the Scottish architect, Colen Campbell, and contains a fine collection of paintings and furniture by the younger Chippendale. The house took a year to build and was one of the first Georgian mansions to be completed. At the north-west of the estate, on Kingsettle Hill, is Alfred's Tower, built in 1772 to commemorate the raising of Alfred's standard here in 878 to rally his troops against the invading Danes.

Walk 18
SPEECH HOUSE AND THE ARBORETUM
FOREST OF DEAN, GLOUCESTERSHIRE
5 miles

Speech House was built in 1676 and is still one of the finest houses in the Forest of Dean. Formerly the King's headquarters in the forest, the house still belongs to the crown but is now leased as an hotel. The former Court Room is now the dining room and can be visited at reasonable times.

The Arboretum has a collection of more than 200 species of trees and shrubs, many of them from China, grown from seeds brought back by a botanist called Wilson. More recently species from North America have been added. Visitors are free to walk round the arboretum, which is open daily, and most of the trees are labelled with species, country of origin and date of planting.

The Forest of Dean is one of the great forests of England and since the days of Edward the Confessor it has been a royal forest, where successive monarchs have hunted for wild boar and deer. It was during the Middle Ages that the Forest of Dean became more important as a source of timber and iron, and it was here that crossbow bolts and horseshoes were fashioned for the English army. Picks, axes, shovels and nails were also forged here for the expedition of Henry II sent to Ireland.

The Forest consists of ten bailiwicks, each with its own bailiff, or Forester-in-Fee. The tomb of one of these bailiffs, with a sculpture of the Forester dressed in hunting costume as the King's bow-bearer, can be seen in All Saints' Church at Newland.

THE SPEECH HOUSE AND ARBORETUM

1 mile

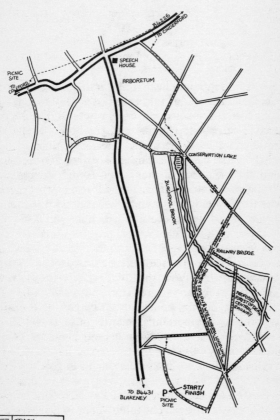

The forest had ceased to be a royal hunting ground by the time Henry VII came to the throne in the late fifteenth century, but its importance as a supplier of timber continued to grow, particularly as it was so close to the West country naval dockyards.

The ownership of the forest passed to Sir John Wintour of Lydney in 1638, when Charles I sold it. The new owner immediately started to fell large stands of trees and enclosed huge areas of the forest. For a time during Cromwell's Commonwealth, the forest was re-nationalised by parliament, but it was restored to Sir John after the restoration to the throne of Charles II.

Because of resentment caused by the large-scale felling, Parliament decreed in 1668 that 11,000 acres of forest should be enclosed and replanted by the Crown, and a further 13,000 acres be protected from felling. The forest was divided into six walks with a keeper's lodge in each.

The staff consisted of the warden, six deputies, foresters and woodwards and four verderers, a post said to have been created by King Canute. Although the forest has undergone many changes in the past few centuries, and is now administered by the Forestry Commission, the titles still remain in force today.

I am grateful to the Forestry Commission and the present warden of the Forest of Dean for being able to use two of their delightful walks which I have slightly modified to produce a figure-of-eight stroll through the trees. You will find places of interest along the way which are numbered to correspond with viewing points recommended by the commission, which supplies a series of guides covering these walks and many others in the forest.

The walk starts at the car park on the right off the B4234 just after it branches off from the B4431 Blakeney to Parkend road. The first leg has been named 'the new Fancy Forest Walk' and is called after the coal mine whose spoil heap – now landscaped – provides the car park. The mine produced about 3½ million tonnes of coal between its opening in 1832 and its closure in 1944. Pit waste was brought by tramway

The railway bridge, now the perfect place to overlook the grazing deer in the Forest of Dean

from the mine and dumped here to form the flat top of the spoil heap. In 1961 two-thirds of the heap was removed for use in the founations of the Llanwern steelworks, and the remainder was landscaped.

The path is clearly signposted and Lime Avenue turns off from the overgrown tramway. The trees were planted about 1810; more recently beech have been planted and these will eventually dominate.

At the intersection of a number of forest rides is the Mineral Loop Line, which used to be operated by the Severn and Wye Railway Company. Opened in 1872, the line had seven miles of track serving the many colleries in the area. At its busiest, in 1912, it was running thirteen trains a day and the last ran on 16 June 1933. The steam trains were a nuisance as their sparks caused many forest fires.

The path continues along the forest road to another intersection which was to have been the route of the Forest of Dean Central Railway line. Unfortunately, the line was abandoned before it ever opened. It was planned to compete with the Severn and Wye Loop but money ran out before all the track could be laid.

During the Second World War many of the forest roads were used by the US army who used the trees as cover for their ammunition dump. Traces of tarmac laid down for the army lorries can still be seen on some of the rides.

The path now leads to the railway bridge, which stands 472 feet above sea level. It is an ideal vantage point from which to spot deer browsing on the rides below. Follow the forest road to the right. Take the first turning left and this will lead you to Speech House Lake and the second loop of the walk. The lake was formed in 1974 by damming the brook which runs for about five miles before joining the Severn. The area is being developed as a wildlife reserve and visitors are asked not to cross the fencing.

The whole of this next loop is waymarked with red arrows on a yellow background. Follow the arrows along the forest road, first across the B4234 and then up to the B4226. This part of the walk takes you through an area of deciduous woodland of beech, sweet chestnut and self-sown hollies. It is Forestry Commission policy to ensure that about half the area of the forest consists of traditional hardwood trees.

On the other side of the B4226 there is the Beechenhurst picnic site, and it too stands on the site of a former coal tip. It was landscaped in 1967 but the poor quality of the land makes it unsuitable for forestry.

The path now follows the road to Speech House and then down to the arboretum. From the arboretum retrace your footsteps back past the lake to the railway bridge to complete the final leg of the return walk to the car.

From the bridge the path now follows the route of the Loop Line but the area has been reclaimed by nature and is very rich both in flora and fauna. The butterfly population is particularly abundant.

The last section of the walk takes you back through the colliery tramways and you can see the massive masonry remains of the gravitation shunting sidings where the trucks used to run downhill under their own weight.

The walk is an ideal chance to see how a forest and industrial culture have co-existed, but how at the end of the day nature is taking over once again.